The Essential
CARNIVORE DIET
Cookbook

60 Delicious Recipes for Healing and Weight Loss

The Essential
CARNIVORE DIET
Cookbook

Vivica Menegaz
Author of *Keto Cooking for Healing and Weight Loss*

Erin Blevins
Founder of shutupEAT

PAGE STREET
PUBLISHING CO.

PAGE STREET
PUBLISHING CO.

TO ALL ANIMALS, WHO HEAL AND
NOURISH OUR BODIES AND ARE SUCH AN
IMPORTANT PART OF THE CYCLE OF LIFE.
WE HONOR YOU!

CONTENTS

LAKE + SEA 99

FOWL 119

STAPLES + SNACKS 135

Foreword

There is a primal, visceral reason we enjoy meat and other animal-based food. It is hard-wired into our biology, because these are the foods that made us who we are as a species. Instead of hiding from who we are and pretending to be herbivores, we should, rather, embrace our biology, and indulging these desires should be celebrated. It's time to get back to our roots as a species.

In order to help us to do so, Vivica Menegaz and Erin Blevins have teamed up to level up the Carnivore culinary game. They have produced a wonderfully packaged collection of truly delicious Carnivore-friendly recipes. The Carnivore dietary approach is rapidly gaining enthusiasm, and more and more people find it to be an incredibly powerful tool in the fight against chronic diseases of all types.

This book cleverly breaks up the recipes by the types of food and by the type of person they are most likely to benefit. Many people use a Carnivore approach for vastly different reasons, and the recipes help to make it easier to tailor the diet appropriately. From Bison Sausage to Succulent Skirt Steak to Roasted Hen with Wild Boar to Branzino al Sale: Salt-Crusted Sea Bass, you are sure to find many delectable favorites.

A Carnivore diet absolutely does not have to be a never-ending series of dry ground beef every day. I highly encourage everyone to indulge themselves and stretch out their culinary wings to make a Carnivore diet not only mouthwatering, but also sustainable over the long term.

Even if your dietary preference leans more to the omnivorous side, you can certainly find many recipes in this book that you are sure to enjoy.

Shawn Baker, MD
CEO of MeatRx.com
Author of *The Carnivore Diet*

Our Stories

In this introduction, we tell you about ourselves and how and why we came to embrace the Carnivore diet.

Vivica

I am Vivica, and I am proud to call myself a holistic practitioner! I am trying to fill in the gaps—big gaps—left open by the medical system when it comes to resolving the root causes of disease. I am the creator of The Healing Foods Method, a very successful nutrition program with a focus on functional endocrinology.

I was born and raised in Italy, and I was lucky, as my childhood was spent in my parents' restaurant, where I learned to appreciate traditional foods like pickled trout and fried brains! My mom taught me how to cook very early, and I always loved anything related to food, from sourcing ingredients to crafting recipes. In my twenties, I lived in three different countries and traveled a lot. I definitely considered myself a food tourist: I was always curious and delighted by local flavors, even the most daring ones.

My love of food also translated to my first career: food photography, where I had the privilege to shoot for magazines like *Gourmet* and *Vanity Fair*.

In my late thirties, I finally encountered nutrition, encouraged by my first mentor, Dr. Deborah Penner, a doctor of chiropractic medicine. I ended up studying with and working for her for five years, until I decided to open my own virtual practice. During those five years, I had some profound realizations: I discovered

I was prediabetic, then I was diagnosed with hypothyroidism with Hashimoto's and then I found out I had fibroids. With my knowledge of nutrition and food, I was able to resolve all of my ailments successfully, especially with the use of a therapeutic ketogenic and Carnivore diet.

My first encounter with the Carnivore diet happened in 2018, through one of my patients. I was fascinated by the idea of an all-meat diet, so I tried it out immediately. I started out consuming only meat, salt and water for about two months. Then, once I felt my gut had adapted to this way of eating, I opened up the diet to include some fruit and low-toxicity vegetables for another couple of months. I felt like the diet made me much stronger and more resilient and that it deeply detoxed my whole organism! Nowadays, my daily diet has a stable foundation of animal proteins and fats, with a small addition of fruits and vegetables. This way of eating evolved as I was first healing my thyroid and deeply detoxing my whole body. The Carnivore way of eating followed my changing needs in the transition to menopause. I also found great support for my hormones—and peace of mind around extra stressful times—by adding in more specific carbs, while still using the base of a Carnivore diet. For the last two years, I have also successfully used the diet in my practice to help many of my patients regain gut-health and recover from a variety of conditions, especially autoimmune disorders.

Erin

"If you can't love your body AND the food you eat, then what's the point?"

My name is Erin Blevins. I'm the founder of shutupEAT and shutupWORK, two companies I have worked under since 2010. shutupEAT gives home chefs and fitness enthusiasts a hands-on experience and a way to follow along while I work, through shutupWORK, with celebrities and pro athletes. I am a special project chef, nutrition coach and project-based private gym co-owner in Salt Lake City, Utah.

I have been in love with food for as long as I can remember. I started cooking at an early age, as an assistant to my highly decorated chef-father, who believes in clean, simple eating and in supporting and promoting local, sustainable farms. By mastering techniques in training, cooking and nutrition, I found a natural way to blend my love of outdoor sports, training and bikini-wearing and enjoying delicious meals.

My skill as a personal chef and nutritional ninja have been used in some of the highest-stakes situations, including the transformation of actor Henry Cavill into a chiseled Superman for DC Film's blockbuster movie *Justice League*. I have served as the chef for intensive team-building retreats for professional baseball teams, like the Atlanta Braves, and I have provided nutrition coaching and cooking for the female freeride development camp for Red Bull Rampage.

This blend of nutritionally dense, delicious cooking and success on some of the world's most competitive stages has kept my passion for a foodie lifestyle alive and thriving. My goal is to embed the knowledge of nutrition and skills of cooking in all my clients. My clientele includes celebrities, elite ultra-marathoners, professional downhill skiers, CrossFit athletes, Major League Baseball players, national weight lifters and Navy SEALs and other US Special Operations Forces members, all of whom strive to feel their best while eating great food. Besides using nutrition for sports performance and aesthetics, I use it as a healing tool to help clients learn to cook better meals for their families, as well as to ease the suffering of those with autoimmune disorders and other degenerative maladies. I use nutritional science as internal medicine. But the real magic in sharing my way of cooking is to bring people together so they can share something incredibly intimate and simple—like a home-cooked meal—with those they love most.

The Carnivore Diet

Why a Carnivore diet? Why any diet? The reasons may be personal, but in general we are all searching for a way to feel better, and we instinctively know that food has something to do with what ails us.

It is easy to say junk food is bad for you. Of course, we should stop overeating sugar and cut out fast food. But often, even when we really try to do what "experts" recommend, we still feel stomach pains and achy joints, and we can't seem to ditch the extra weight.

As health practitioners, nothing is more frustrating for us than to see those trying to help themselves trusting the latest diet trends, yet failing to achieve their goals of radiating health and well-being. It's also frustrating to see the despair and sense of helplessness that results. For those who have struggled with diets in the past, we have an answer for you.

The Carnivore diet is a powerful, nutritional therapy that can help reset the body, promote healing and give people the power to control their own well-being through the process of elimination. Once we eliminate processed and other inflammatory foods, we are able to add back in the whole foods that heal the gut and prepare the body to absorb nutrition again. In our practice, we have observed that people with severe intolerances and metabolic disorders can give their bodies the nutrition they need to heal on their own. This happens when people choose the right foods and eliminate disease-causing ones.

We look at this process from the very origin of humanity. We look at what nourished our ancestors and what our bodies were designed to use as the main source of fuel before agriculture started. We come back to the first food: meat.

To us, meat is magic; it is medicine. High-quality meat is the most nutrient-dense food on the planet. It is part of our history, our lineage. Our ancestors understood the importance of meat and adorned their caves with depictions of the hunt. Meat was the subject of the first known human artistic expression, and we will show you how to make your dinner art!

The Essential Carnivore Diet Cookbook is a practical therapeutic system and protocol for those wishing to become more independent with their own health and nutrition.

The way the Carnivore diet works is based on a simple concept: eliminate the plant materials loaded with phytotoxins, and provide all the necessary nutrients through animal-based foods. What are phytotoxins, you might ask? They are the chemical weapons plants use to defend themselves from bugs and animals trying to eat them. You might have heard talk of harmful lectins or oxalates. Those are just two examples of the many toxic chemicals that plants employ, and they can cause harm to the human organism.

In addition, we need to consider that nutrients coming from plants are not readily absorbed by the human digestive system because of those protective barriers. Animal-based foods require very little effort for our bodies to break them down and absorb their nutrients. Plant matter needs a series of high-energy, biochemical processes to first make them less harmful, then put them to good use. Therefore, by removing inflammatory and damaging plant-based foods, we give our body the opportunity to start healing and be fully nourished!

In the next chapter, find the Carnivore style most suitable for you, then follow the recipes for that style and the results will speak for themselves! Healing and thriving can be simple.

Applications of the Carnivore Diet

Here we discuss the various applications of the Carnivore diet and how it interacts with weight loss, weight gain, physical activity, female hormones, gut-healing and kids. We also go over how to use the diet for both gut-healing and weight loss, and advise on how best to use the Carnivore diet and carbohydrates for performance during intense training.

Carnivore and Weight Loss

It is common knowledge that there is more to weight loss than calories eaten and calories burned. What are the mysteries of metabolism that need to be unveiled for successful, long-lasting weight loss, and how can the Carnivore diet help?

Some of the main issues in the western world today are obesity, defined as excessive accumulation and storage of fat in the body, and metabolic syndrome, which is marked by the presence of three or more of a group of factors—such as high blood pressure, abdominal obesity, high triglyceride levels, low HDL levels and high fasting levels of blood sugar. The syndrome is linked to increased risk of cardiovascular

disease and type 2 diabetes. These problems have been driven by the excess number of calories consumed in combination with sedentary lifestyles, but the main cause is the change of diet ushered in by manipulated science. This led to years of fat-shaming, starting in 1955 with Ancel Keys and his aggressively pushed theory that fat, not sugar, was the culprit for cardiovascular disease.

As diets became depleted of healthy, nutritious fats, sugar and refined carbohydrates took their place. Consuming such carbohydrates causes blood glucose levels to spike, which in turn causes the release of insulin, the storage hormone. Insulin pushes glucose out of the bloodstream and into the liver and the muscles as glycogen, or to be stored as fat. Perpetually high insulin levels in the blood eventually lead to metabolic syndrome and insulin resistance. In addition, the nutrient density of foods plummeted, and people started eating large amounts of empty calories, especially in the form of sugar, which further depletes the body of nutrients.

People became malnourished, even in the presence of an apparent abundance of food. The extreme high-carb content combined with a lack of nutrients creates a series of dysfunctional hormonal loops, starting with the fat-storage hormone insulin, as we just saw. When insulin is dysregulated for long periods of time, it starts affecting other hormones as well, like the hunger-regulating hormones leptin and ghrelin, and even the stress hormone cortisol. This chain reaction ends up negatively affecting blood glucose, energy levels and the ability to feel satiated. A low-fat/high-carb diet creates a vicious loop of always hungry/never nourished/always overweight.

The Carnivore diet is the perfect way to fix insulin resistance and malnutrition. High fat, high protein and no carbs will quickly restore receptor cells to insulin sensitivity and eventually bring hunger hormones back into balance. Protein is especially healing to dysregulated hunger hormones, as it is the most satiating of all the macros. ("Macros" is short for "macro-nutrients," referring to carbs, fats and protein—the three basic components of every diet.) In addition, there are no empty calories on the Carnivore diet, especially when following our Nutrient-Dense Style (see page 24). Eating the Carnivore way will reverse and heal much of the damage done by high-carb diets.

Let's look at other common reasons for weight gain/inability to lose weight. The most probable one is toxicity. Toxins accumulate in the fat tissues as the body's detoxification pathways, such as the liver and kidney, become overwhelmed and congested. Inability to release the toxins forces the body to retain fat as the only safe storage place. Some examples of easily accumulated toxins are heavy metals; glyphosates, or herbicides; pesticides; chemicals; food additives; and preservatives. Our Purist Style (see page 23) can help significantly in this case, because it's an extreme elimination diet and supports the body's natural ability to detox.

The body can also become toxic with excess hormones. The toxicity could start with high insulin, as we saw above, and then progress to high cortisol, high estrogen, high testosterone, etc. The Carnivore diet helps this by reducing exogenous hormones from foods, especially when eating nose-to-tail, organic, pastured animals and by providing all the nutrients needed for successful detoxification. Protein is especially needed for detoxing, as toxins need an amino acid carrier in order to be excreted through the gut or kidney pathways.

When we look at the best ways of eating for weight loss, something to keep in mind is that the body prioritizes certain energy sources due to the availability of storage. Carbs have a limited storage space, so the body will always prioritize carbs as fuel. Fat has an unlimited storage potential, so, in order for the body to prioritize fat as an energy source, we need to reduce the presence of carbohydrates, even in a calorie-deficit scenario. So, the first step for weight loss will be to reduce carbohydrates enough to induce a state of nutritional ketosis, a natural metabolic state in which your body is fueled mainly by fats and ketones, instead of glucose. That is why the Purist Style (see page 23) and Nutrient-Dense Style (see page 24) diets are recommended for weight loss. In addition, depending on your weight-loss needs, you can accomplish the needed calorie deficit by reducing your fat calories by up to 20 percent.

Another significant benefit of using the Carnivore diet for weight loss is due to the Thermic Effect of Feeding, or TEF. Different foods have different thermic effects, which is the number of calories burned in order to digest that food. Protein has the highest TEF of all foods. In addition, Carnivore diets should be mostly ketogenic, adding the benefits of ketosis for maximum fat-burning ability! If you're considering using the Carnivore diet for weight loss and to heal a sluggish metabolism, use macro ratios that induce ketosis and follow the Purist (see page 23) or Nutrient-Dense (see page 24) Styles for maximum benefit.

We can reduce fat calories to lose weight, but once the desired weight is achieved, the ratio of fat to protein should be around 1:1. Long-term focus on lean protein will cause nutritional imbalances in the body, as protein is designed to be a building block, not a source of energy.

To help stimulate metabolism and aid weight loss in particularly difficult cases, you can do some macros cycling or rotate the macronutrient ratios.

Do You Need Gut-Healing and Weight Loss?

If you need gut-healing in addition to weight loss, do the following:

- Set your macros at 30 percent protein and 70 percent fat at X number of calories. You can use any macros calculator to determine how many calories you need. We like to use a simple one: keto-calculator.ankerl.com.

- Monday, Wednesday and Friday: Eat your normal macros, with normal calories.

- Tuesday and Thursday: Eat only lean protein at the equivalent of your normal calories.

- Saturday and Sunday: Do two high-fat days, where you eat 90 percent fat and half of your regular calories.

This way of eating is not recommended for the long term. It's helpful for periods of weight loss, used for a maximum of a month at a time.

Carnivore and Weight Gain

If you are trying to build overall mass and gain weight on a Carnivore diet, you may be slightly disappointed, unless you execute a diligent plan and stay in a caloric excess for a consistent amount of time while training. Maintaining lean muscle and lowering your body fat to a more natural composition is a more likely outcome. With that being said, gaining weight is not impossible on the diet. To gain weight on any dietary structure, you have to first be in caloric excess, which means you are giving your body more calories than it is able to burn during the day. To figure out your number, simply track calorie intake for a week or two to determine at what calorie level you are maintaining your current body weight. Then, add 6 to 10 percent of your number in calories per week until you reach your desired weight.

Very few see a fat gain on the Carnivore diet, but if you increase your calorie intake too fast, you may see some body-fat storage. To combat this, simply dial back or stop your calorie increase for a week or two, then resume the increase once your body has adjusted to the extra calories.

Carnivore and Physical Activity

Our Ancestral Style (see page 25) of the Carnivore diet is the most beneficial Carnivore style for sports performance. With that being said, you can make any of the Carnivore styles work, with consideration to the adjustment phase. The Carnivore diet is a high-protein, high-fat structured way of eating, which can be great for some sports but not as ideal for others. There is ongoing research into the performance benefits of a high-fat, moderate-protein, low-carbohydrate (keto) approach to athletic performance that shows some promise in some sports.

The best applications tend to be in endurance sports of longer duration, but also some strength sports. Athletic and sports performance on a Carnivore diet requires an adaptation period depending on training history, volume and carb dependency. This can be addressed with the use of honey and some fruit in most cases, as demonstrated in the Ancestral Style (see page 25) of the Carnivore diet.

It is necessary to give enough time for proper adaptation to occur. This sometimes manifests as extreme lethargy, called the keto flu, for the first few weeks of a low-carb diet. It is very apparent in athletes, who have greater energetic demands and generally have a sensitivity to their energy levels. A few things can help during this period: mainly, paying attention to electrolyte balance—specifically sodium and potassium, but also magnesium—as exercise volume and intensity increases. Intentionally increasing fat intake can also improve symptoms.

How to Use Carbohydrates for Performance

If you are practicing regular activity, such as walking, biking to work or hiking, you will adapt quite well to any of the Carnivore styles outlined in this book. However, if you are recovering from longer physical efforts, such as circuit-training intensity or weight lifting, you may consider adopting the Ancestral Style (see page 25) as a means for recovery and performance. As you read through the Ancestral Style, you will see we have incorporated a few sources of carbohydrates: berries or a limited amount of fruit and honey. This is plenty to recover glycogen stores and fuel effort, with just a slight increase in carbohydrates. We have listed a few examples of how to program carbohydrates around effort.

For short- to medium-duration—30 to 90 minutes—endurance efforts, you can train fasted. If you are efficient with the activity, recover with a meal afterward. If you are adding any type of intensity—think of your heart rate above 75 percent of your maximum heart rate—you may want to consume somewhere in the range of 25 to 45 grams of carbohydrates 30 to 60 minutes prior to your effort, depending on how fast you digest food. This will give you some glycogen to burn during your effort, allowing performance to remain high during training; add in a little coffee, and you should have a great training session. If you are weight training—lifting above 70 percent of 1-rep maximum—then treat it the same as the intense training listed above.

Depending on the duration and style of training, you may be able to train fasted. But, if you are more focused on maximum weight on the bar or intense acidic states required for hypertrophy and muscle-building, then you will want to have essential amino acids from protein sources, along with glycogen—carbohydrates—in the system to maximize your sessions. Adding about 30 to 50 grams of carbohydrates and 20 to 50 grams of protein 30 to 60 minutes prior to training can really enhance your ability to recover from intense training.

Recovering on the Carnivore diet adopts similar rules to normal sports recovery. Your body needs carbohydrates to maximize protein synthesis and a small amount of protein to mend broken-down muscle tissue. Luckily, parts of the Carnivore diet, along with intermittent fasting, help keep most people in a parasympathetic state. This is a state of the nervous system in which your body has the best ability to repair itself; it's ideal for recovering. You will benefit from lower fat and protein sources during the recovery window—immediately following training and up to 2 hours—and about 20 to 50 grams of carbohydrates after training. We have listed a range because, as you are on the diet for longer periods of time, you will become more efficient with the small amounts of carbohydrates you give your body, and you will need less to get the job done. The same goes for protein; we become more efficient the older and more experienced at training we get.

A good test is to start with 25 grams of carbs pre- and post-training. If you feel great the next day, it was enough. If you get through your training week and feel fatigued or sore, take a rest day, recover with a mineral complex and add a day of eating slightly more carbohydrates so you can get back to training rested and recovered. If you are going to add in carbohydrates for physical activity or performance, as suggested in the Ancestral Style section (see page 25), feel free to use carbohydrates near training. The further you get from physical activity, cut back on carbohydrates to avoid storing unneeded fuel.

Carnivore and Female Hormones

A Carnivore diet can be a great aid in resolving certain hormonal issues for women. Here are some examples:

Polycystic ovary syndrome, or PCOS, is a condition driven by high estrogen and high testosterone. PCOS is also a disease that causes high insulin and a congested liver. As we mentioned in the section on weight loss (see page 14), detoxing excess hormones is greatly supported by a nose-to-tail Purist Style Carnivore diet (see page 23). This way of eating also helps lower insulin and lose weight, addressing the main healing points for PCOS.

Menorrhagia, which is heavy periods with clots, is also driven by high estrogen and helped by a Carnivore diet. In addition, eating the Nutrient-Dense Style (see page 24) will help replenish precious iron, preventing anemia from blood loss.

Within the topic of hormones, we need to give special attention to the specific issues of **perimenopause**, the period around the onset of menopause. As hormones start shifting, the body's needs are also changing.

Where in the previous examples we talked about problems that might arise in the reproductive years, in perimenopause we are looking at a very different scenario. The ovaries' production of hormones is slowly declining, and the adrenal glands are starting to gradually take over. Adrenal support becomes of prime importance if we want to maintain balance. Calorie restriction and extreme carbohydrate restriction are always considered stressors by the female body. When in perimenopause, we need to be mindful of every added stress put on the adrenal glands, as it might push the body to imbalance and become symptomatic.

To help achieve a healthy perimenopause, we recommend adding some cyclical carbohydrates to the Carnivore diet to help relieve hormonal symptoms, such as insomnia, fatigue and mood swings.

In our experience, the best way to do this is to use the Ancestral Style (see page 25) of the diet and to add carbs to the last meal of the day about two to four times a week. Depending on the individual, an amount from 50 to 200 grams of carbs can be beneficial.

Carnivore and Gut-Healing

There are several reasons why the Carnivore diet is the perfect way to heal the gut, especially gut permeability, and consequently heal all conditions generated by gut dysfunction. The number one reason is that the Carnivore diet doesn't contain the very substances that cause leaky gut: food additives and plant toxins. The second important reason is that the Carnivore diet is a nutrient-dense diet and provides all the elements needed for the body to heal and rebuild the gut lining. The third reason is that the Carnivore diet leverages the benefits of ketosis, which are derived both from low and stable insulin and from the anti-inflammatory properties of ketosis itself.

When gut-healing is the priority, it is important to focus on sufficient fat and connective tissue intake. The connective tissue can be in the form of collagen, powder or gelatin. We strongly recommend making your own healing broth high in gelatin by adding beef feet and tendons to the Beef Bone Marrow Broth recipe (see page 67).

Carnivore and Kids

Most kids already have a taste for meat from an early age, and they greatly benefit from the energy-dense and nutrient-dense clean foods of the Carnivore way of eating. If you start early with your children, it becomes an easy transition toward ancestral foods like mountain berries, fatty, organic grass-fed meats and ghee. We encourage kids to eat more like their healthy parents than like kids eating a typical processed-food diet. Children's health is very important, and kids need to be exposed to good nutrition at an early age so they can have the best opportunity at healthy development and disease prevention! Just think about the child obesity and diabetes epidemics; a mostly Carnivore diet for kids could be an uncomplicated solution to such daunting issues. We also understand that most kids can tolerate more carbohydrates than adults, so they don't need to be as strict as their parents.

Make your Carnivore foods for kids taste delicious and look appetizing; offer options like berry smoothies, nutritious soup broths and steak strips. If your child is extremely active, make sure they are getting enough sleep, electrolytes and plenty of carbohydrates from healthy sources. As diet changes can be difficult sometimes, if you are trying to switch older children to a mostly Carnivore lifestyle, make sure you do so gradually and with lots of patience. Children need a wide variety of nutrition, and—if they are exposed to Carnivore options as the majority of their caloric intake—they are more likely to be drawn toward healthy options in the future, whether they adopt Carnivore or not.

Important Considerations

It is important to be aware of the role salt, iodine, dairy foods, organ meats and intermittent fasting have in a successful application of the Carnivore diet.

Salt

Electrolytes are a very important factor to consider when starting a Carnivore diet. When carbohydrate consumption is limited or eliminated, the body will flush a considerable quantity of fluid from the cells, as well as electrolytes, especially sodium. In order to avoid unnecessary symptoms, like the famous keto flu, it's important to supplement with enough sodium. This is especially true when first transitioning from a higher-carb diet to Carnivore. In this case, we recommend about 5 to 10 grams of sodium a day. One teaspoon (15 g) of fine sea salt contains an average of 2 grams of sodium.

A great way to add electrolytes naturally is to drink bone and meat broth!

Another important point is that not all salt is created equal. We recommend using fine, unrefined salt rich in trace minerals from clean sources. Redmond Real Salt and Celtic Sea Salt are two of our favorite salts.

Iodine

Iodine is a necessary nutrient, one whose importance has been largely undervalued, mostly due to the advent of chemical drugs. Iodine is necessary for the production of thyroid hormones, and, in our opinion, iodine deficiency is one of the driving factors of the hypothyroidism epidemic. When following the Carnivore diet for long periods of time—6 months or longer—we recommend supplementing with an atomic iodine supplement in a base of glycerin. Atomic iodine consists of a single atom of negatively charged iodine, or I-, which is easily absorbed into the cells without the need for potassium iodide. Dosage depends on the needs of the individual; we recommend working with a knowledgeable nutritionist.

Dairy

There are different opinions about consuming dairy on a Carnivore diet. Dairy can be an easy and inexpensive source of fat and protein, but, in our opinion, the benefits are not worth the harm it creates. Dairy can be a powerfully addictive combination of fat and carbohydrates. In addition, it contains proteins, called beta-casomorphins, that activate the opioid-signaling pathways of the brain, reinforcing its addictive properties. Dairy is a food designed to grow a baby into a large adult; therefore, it contains the elements for weight gain and mass gain. It also naturally contains powerful hormones, which interfere with a woman's own delicate hormone balance.

We recommend not using dairy as part of your Carnivore lifestyle, with the exception of ghee. Ghee that has been sourced from grass-fed cows is low in toxins, and it can be a good way to add fat to the diet without adding the dangerous proteins of milk. Of course, we recommend an organic, grass-fed product; make sure it is casein free.

Organ Meats

Why did we include so many organ-meat recipes? We believe that a healing diet should be rich in bioavailable nutrients and low in toxins. That is why plant-based diets are not ideal, because plants protect themselves from being eaten with phytotoxins. Most plants considered nutritious today are in fact full of antinutrients, substances that block the assimilation of actual vitamins and minerals. So where do the most absorbable nutrients actually come from? They come from different parts of the animal. In Chinese medicine, it is said to "eat the organ you need to heal." This makes sense, as that very organ will contain all the necessary nutrients to feed itself, plus healthy DNA to help cellular replication.

Though our recipes in this book are limited to including the liver and heart, we strongly recommend extending your experiments with organ meats to other delicious parts, such as the kidneys, thymus, brains and lungs. All these parts are eaten in every traditional and ancestral diet. Not only were no parts wasted, the organs were consumed first or saved for pregnant women and elderly people. For those of you who are not as taste-adventurous as we are, we recommend at least including liver in whatever version of the Carnivore diet you choose.

Intermittent Fasting

Intermittent fasting seems to be a buzzword these days. But don't let the hype distract from the real potential of using it as a way to increase energy and cognitive ability, as well as help in healing your gut and making it easier to control food intake.

There are some real technical benefits to intermittent fasting, such as autophagy, or cellular recycling, and hormonal balancing. But we find that the complicated benefits deter people who are interested in trying intermittent fasting and are having a hard time understanding why it could help them. Here are some really easy ways to incorporate the concept without needing a PhD in nutritional science.

Pick an eating and fasting window. The most common is a 16/8. This means that you will fast 16 hours and then have 8 hours in which to eat normally. Don't let the numbers fool you. It sounds a bit intimidating at first—like you will experience some major hunger pains—but we find that most busy people fall into this schedule really easily. If you finish dinner around 8 or 9 pm like most people, it means you will go to bed pretty satiated. When you wake up, have some water and black coffee; some feel like adding a little ghee or collagen powder helps at first to adapt to the fast. Go to work or get a training session in before heading to the office. Around 1 or 2 pm, have your first meal. Voilà! You are intermittent fasting.

As you adapt to fasting, you can shorten the eating window to something like 19/5 or even just one meal every 24 hours. But don't feel like you have to be super strict with the time; if you get hungry, eat!

The real benefits are quite simple. Not having to think about food or your next meal will allow you to concentrate on more important things. Productivity goes up because the more you fast, the more your body creates ketone bodies to fuel your brain, which increases cognition and has a helpful appetite-suppression effect.

"Wait, are you saying the more I go hungry, the less I will be hungry?"

Yes!

This effect is well studied. This break from food also allows you to minimize your total intake, which is an easy way to start dropping some extra body fat if you have it.

Although fasting has some serious health benefits, one that will be apparent almost immediately is the break you give to your digestive system. This allows time and resources to repair other issues going on internally. It is common for people to report better hair and nail growth, less creaky joints and even faster recovery between training sessions.

People who practice the Carnivore diet usually fall into a natural intermittent schedule by default because of how satiating the meals are. Plus, the nutrient density also tends to stave off cravings and snacking that people normally feel on a mostly carbohydrate diet that had them eating six times a day.

Intermittent fasting is a great way to free up some time to do other things besides think about, prepare and clean up after food prep. Incorporate it a few days to start, and allow yourself time to adjust when you feel you need to.

What's Your Carnivore Style?

Although there is only one Carnivore diet, there are different styles you can use to make the most out of it, depending on your needs and goals. What we call styles are actually different levels of elimination, going from strictest to more lenient, that can address healing specific ailments or be used for a long-term lifestyle. Let us explain and break it down for you!

The Purist Style

Red meat from ruminants and salt only.

This version of Carnivore is an elimination diet for healing and rapid weight loss and should not be followed for more than six months, because it lacks some essential nutrients.

What to Eat: Beef, bison, lamb, sheep, goat, venison, elk, moose. Coffee is allowed in moderation once health is restored. Sea or Himalayan salt.

Most Helpful For: People who suffer from autoimmune conditions, such as Crohn's disease, ulcerative colitis and rheumatoid arthritis, or gastrointestinal issues, such as irritable bowel syndrome, or IBS, and small intestinal bacterial overgrowth, or SIBO. This style is best for weight-loss stalls induced by toxicity.

Benefits: It's the easiest way to do a nutrient-rich elimination diet and is designed to heal the most difficult conditions. Most meals are easy to prepare and absolutely delicious. This style is also budget-friendly.

To feel the power of what food can do for your body and well-being, we find it useful to get to the root of the problem by taking away possible antagonists and stripping food down to its most necessary form. The transition from modern eating to a pure Carnivore diet takes time. However, once your body acclimates, you will start to heal your body from the inside out.

The Purist Style is just that, food brought back to its most fundamental: meat, salt and water! Simplicity doesn't mean your food has to be boring. Here is your chance to perfect a meaningful main dish and learn how to craft perfectly prepared meats that will heal and nourish your body.

We address variety in the Purist method by adding diversity in how to prepare meats with salt. This seems simple enough, but the assortment of meats and preparation styles will keep the Purist's palate intrigued meal after meal. This is fundamental to making this therapy sustainable until your body can heal. This is the perfect place to start if you struggle with autoimmune disorders, Crohn's, multiple food allergies, food intolerances, acid reflux, poor digestion, low energy, lethargy, poor cognitive performance, poor sleeping habits, hormone imbalance or excess weight. Once you see how this method works with your system, you can add foods in as you feel necessary to accomplish your health goals.

The Purist Style may not be ideal for the avid athlete training often at a high intensity, especially during the initial time period when you're adjusting to the diet. But once you adapt, you will be able to better understand what your energy levels look like and how to navigate from there.

One tip while learning how to incorporate this style of the Carnivore diet into your physical activity is to shorten the duration of your training sessions and see how your body recovers from the effort. Then, add duration and intensity as you see fit.

Training earlier in the day fasted will allow your body to move without the extra stress from digesting and breaking down food. You will then recover after your training with a meal or snack.

The Nutrient-Dense Style

Red meat, pork, organ meats, poultry, fish, seafood, eggs, ghee and salt.

This version of the diet contains all the necessary nutrients, so it can be followed long term. It is still a powerful elimination diet, and it can be the perfect sequel to the Purist Style if you started there and are now adding in a few foods that may be beneficial.

What to Eat: Beef, bison, lamb, sheep, goat, venison, elk, moose, boar, pork (in moderation and organic only), all kinds of fish and shellfish, all poultry, eggs, fish eggs. Organic ghee from grass-fed cows. Coffee is allowed in moderation once health is restored. Sea or Himalayan salt.

Most Helpful For: Men and women experiencing fertility issues; people with thyroid and adrenal hormone imbalances; people with anxiety and depression, Alzheimer's, epilepsy or seizures and other brain issues; and people with inflammation and arthritis.

About Dairy and the Nutrient-Dense Style

Carnivore is a healing diet for us. It's a way of eating targeted at reducing inflammation. We consider most dairy foods highly inflammatory, especially nonorganic, pasteurized and homogenized products whose nutritional properties and convenience don't justify the risk of the issues and sensitivities they might cause. Organic ghee from grass-fed cows is a beneficial inclusion in the diet. It's included with the Nutrient-Dense Style because of the nutritional benefits and versatility it offers. It also adds a great deal of flavor to other foods in this style.

Benefits: This style includes all of the nutrients a human needs to thrive, if you eat enough organ meats, so that you will not need to add them as supplements. This diet can be sustained indefinitely. It's an easy and uncomplicated way of eating, with an extra variety of ingredients, that still functions as a healing and elimination diet suitable for a variety of ailments.

We included a wide variety of meats in this Carnivore style for people who may struggle with digestion, anxiety or hormonal issues or have limited access to red meat. This style of the diet also includes eggs, ghee, fish and poultry, so it's a great place to start if you want to restrict your foods gradually.

If you find you would benefit from higher energy levels or you are trying to exercise and not recovering well after the one-month adaptation period, you may want to try the Ancestral Style instead.

The Ancestral Style

Red fatty meat, pork, organ meats, eggs, fish and shellfish, fat, ghee, salt, some fruit and honey in extreme moderation.

This version of the diet includes some carbohydrates, which can be beneficial for women with hormonal issues, especially during perimenopause, and for athletes. This version is also ideal for the long term, as it adds variety and the ability to carb-up.

What to Eat: Beef, bison, lamb, sheep, goat, venison, elk, moose, boar, pork (in extreme moderation and organic only), all kinds of fish and shellfish, all poultry, eggs, fish eggs. Organic ghee from grass-fed cows. Coffee is allowed in moderation once health is restored. Sea or Himalayan salt. Local and seasonal fruits in moderation, especially low-sugar fruits like berries. Honey in extreme moderation.

Most Helpful For: Women in perimenopause and transitioning to menopause, athletes and anybody who wants to expand their diet after achieving the desired healing from the Purist or Nutrient-Dense styles.

Benefits: This style is easy to follow, with a delicious and varied way of eating, without the perils of inflammatory foods. It offers the ability to modulate some carbs to help with hormonal changes and athletic performance.

The Ancestral Style of the Carnivore diet is the most liberal form of the styles in this book. We have added foods for specific reasons, such as carbohydrates for physical activity and hormone balancing. This is also a great style for kids to experiment with. The Ancestral Style adds wild mountain berries, a limited amount of fruits and honey to the Carnivore diet. This style of the diet can be used to fuel performance, recover from physical activity and balance out energy levels for those with an active lifestyle as it is better explained in the chapter about carbs and performance (see page 13).

Macros

We can c
of Carniv
found in
energy
amino a
neogen
energy
We nee
blocks
the fu

What is the ideal ratio of fat to p
perfect ratio will be unique to our individual needs. In general, we can have two different priorities: energy or building blocks.

For children, elderly people or those who want to build muscle, calculate your protein need at 1.2 grams per pound of body weight.

For muscle maintenance, weight loss and to support an average activity level, calculate your protein need at 1 gram per pound of body weight.

Then calculate how many grams of fat you need based on your calorie needs, using a keto macro calculator such as keto-calculator.ankerl.com. The macros will look approximately like this:

- 0 percent carbohydrates, 30 percent protein and 70 percent fat.

For the Ancestral Style, use the same protein-need calculation as explained above, and use these macros:

- 5 percent carbs, 30 percent protein and 65 percent fat.

It's helpful to input the percentages you calculate into a macro tracking app, such as MyFitnessPal, to track your progress in following the Carnivore diet.

Troubleshooting

In the process of adapting to the Carnivore diet, some issues can arise. Here are tips for how to handle constipation, dehydration, hot flashes and amenorrhea.

Constipation and Diarrhea

Gut-healing is probably the number one reason to adopt a Carnivore diet, but during the transition from any other kind of diet to Carnivore, the gut will need time to adapt. During this adaptation period, you might remain symptomatic or the severity of symptoms can increase. This adaptation time is needed as the fiber-digesting bacteria slowly decrease in numbers, while the meat-digesting bacteria increase and take over the microbiome.

One of the most common digestive symptoms when first starting this diet is diarrhea. Diarrhea can be caused by the sudden increase in fat consumed, as the body needs time to start producing more fat enzymes, or lipase, and bile to emulsify it. Diarrhea can also be due to a too-high protein content relative to fat. Depending on your unique gut composition, you might need to reduce the fat or potentially reduce the protein if diarrhea occurs. Usually the gut-adaptation will not take longer than two weeks.

Constipation can also happen when transitioning from a diet containing fiber to the fiber-free Carnivore diet. For people who have become fiber intolerant, switching to a Carnivore diet will relieve constipation. People used to large amounts of roughage in their diets will experience a sudden reduction and slow down of bowel movements.

It's to be expected that the volume and frequency of BMs will be reduced when one is on the Carnivore diet; nonstraining bowel movements two to three times a week should be perfectly acceptable. Meat is mostly absorbed in the small intestine, so not much will reach the colon and part of your fecal matter will actually be your microbiome's poop.

Here are some things to try when experiencing constipation on the Carnivore diet:

- Increase hydration by adding a pinch of Redmond Real Salt or Celtic Sea Salt to every quart of water you drink.

- Drink bone broth daily to increase hydration.

- Add fat and lower your protein intake until the problem resolves.

What I, Vivica, have also experienced in my clinical practice is that people who need gut-healing and become fiber-intolerant will do great on the Carnivore diet until the gut lining is restored to integrity. Then, suddenly, they will develop constipation. Those people can usually transition to the Ancestral Style of Carnivore or a Keto Paleo diet to relieve the constipation.

Dehydration

Dehydration is not an issue specific to the Carnivore diet, but a common one for many people. I, Vivica, read blood work every day where multiple markers for dehydration are present. In my opinion, it is especially important to be aware of dehydration while on a Carnivore diet because it can be an important factor in the reduced production of hydrochloric, or stomach, acid which is of paramount importance for the breakdown and absorption of proteins. I recommend that my patients drink about eight ounces (240 ml) of water mixed with one-quarter teaspoon of salt about 30 minutes before meals. This will not only help hydrate the body, but also prepare the digestive juices.

Hot Flashes

Sometimes, starting a Carnivore diet will activate hot flashes in perimenopausal women or reactivate them in postmenopausal women, even after years of not having them. Hot flashes are an unpleasant phenomenon caused by the fluctuating levels of hormones, especially declining levels of estrogen, or estradiol, and increasing levels of follicle-stimulating hormone, or FSH. Hot flashes are modulated by the hypothalamus, and they can be triggered by excess cortisol, the stress hormone, in the body or by external temperature fluctuations. They are a quick way for the body to get rid of excess heat as hormones fluctuate.

To understand the correlation between hot flashes and protein consumption, we need to go back to the concept of the Thermic Effect of Feeding, or TEF. As we saw in the section about weight loss (see page 14), different macronutrients carry different thermic potentials. Protein is the macro with the highest TEF, which means that it requires a lot of energy to break down, and consuming protein actually raises metabolism and the ability to burn calories for energy. As the body consumes protein, it burns more energy, and one way to expend that energy is to burn hotter, which in turn can stimulate the hypothalamus response and trigger a hot flash. So yes, it's actually a good thing. But hot flashes are not pleasant, so what can you do about it?

In our opinion, the best thing to do is support the liver through proper supplementation. During the transition to a fully Carnivore diet, this is best achieved with the help of a professional. Once adapted to the higher protein content, your body should normalize to the increased ability to burn calories and convert them to energy. The liver is the center of hormone detoxification, so it plays a very important role in clearing excess and maintaining healthy levels.

Amenorrhea

When it comes to hormones, diet is not always enough to regulate underlying, long-standing dysfunctions. One of the pre-existing conditions that could be either resolved or sometimes aggravated by the Carnivore diet is amenorrhea, or lack of menstrual cycles.

Here are two different scenarios that can cause the loss of periods when following the Carnivore diet:

Case 1: A healthy woman with well-balanced hormones follows a very low-calorie, low-fat Carnivore diet while on an intense physical training schedule for too long. The reduction in calories and body fat, combined with high cortisol levels from intense exercise, will likely impact female hormones to the point of losing ovulatory cycles, resulting in missed periods.

Case 2: A woman with pre-existing issues, which caused her hormonal imbalances, starts the Carnivore diet to help get her periods back, but instead of resolving the issue, the diet aggravates it.

To resolve case 1, add in more calories and more fat and, possibly, add strategic carbohydrates. Adding carbohydrates, as in the Ancestral Style, will be beneficial for women who are not dealing with autoimmunity or digestive disorders.

In case 2, we need to address the underlying root causes as well as correct the diet to resolve the problem. Here are some of the most common underlying issues:

- Adrenal fatigue from chronic stress or over-exercising.

- Malnutrition from a low-fat or low-nutrients diet.

- Extreme calorie restriction.

While those issues are addressed, we recommend starting with a less restrictive Carnivore style, like the Ancestral Style. Once periods are restored, it will be possible to successfully transition to a stricter style, if desired.

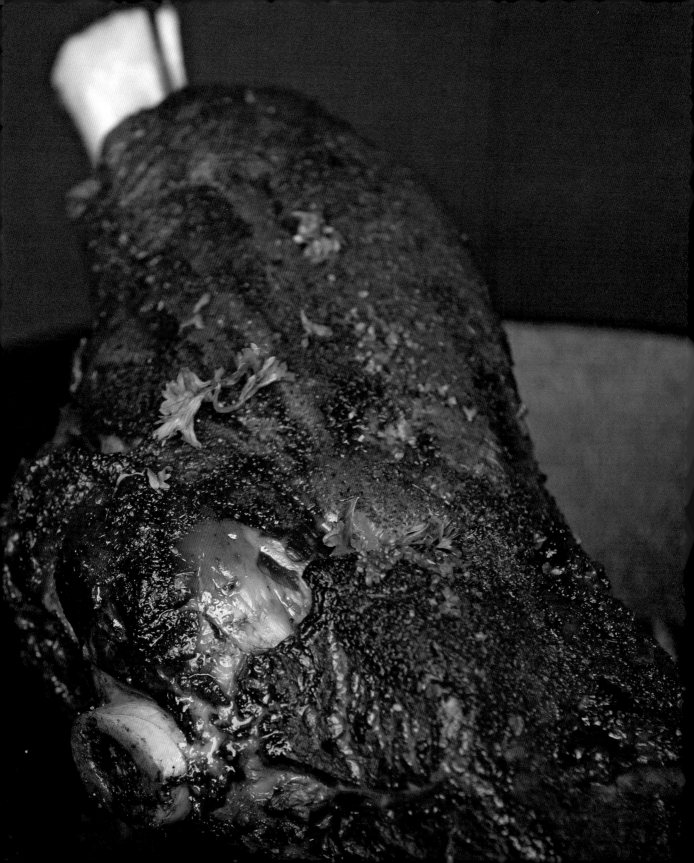

RED MEAT + WILD GAME

Carnivore Steak Tartare

NUTRIENT-DENSE STYLE

Yields 4 servings
Per Serving:
Calories 299
Fat 18 g
Protein 31 g
Carbs 0.25 g

For this recipe, the quality of the ingredients is what matters most, not only from the nutritional value standpoint, but also for the best flavor! Make sure you get the highest quality beef you can find. We recommend using grass-fed, grass-finished beef, never frozen, and custom cut by a butcher. For the egg, use the freshest, pasture-raised hen eggs you can find; you will not regret it!

1 lb (455 g) fresh grass-fed beef tenderloin

1 organic egg yolk

1 tsp Herb-Infused Salt (see page 139)

Chill the tenderloin in the freezer for 15 minutes to firm up the meat before it's sliced. Also chill the bowl and plates you will use to mix and serve the tartare.

Remove the meat from the freezer. With a very sharp chef's knife, cut the tenderloin into ⅛-inch (4-mm) slices. Then, stacking a few slices at a time, cut the tenderloin into ⅛-inch (4-mm)-thin strips. Finally, cut the strips into ⅛-inch (4-mm) cubes, a few strips at a time.

Place the beef cubes in the chilled bowl, add the egg yolk and the salt and mix until the ingredients are well blended.

Serve the tartare on the chilled plates, and eat it immediately.

Nutrition Notes

You will benefit most from this recipe if you have an autoimmune condition, a digestive disorder or any gastrointestinal issues. Raw protein is in its most digestible form. You will love this recipe if you want to lose weight and adapt quickly to this way of life.

Smoky Carpaccio with Golden Marrow Oil

PURIST STYLE

As with the tartare (see page 32), you will not want to skimp on the quality of your meat for this recipe. We recommend using grass-fed, grass-finished beef, never frozen, and custom cut by a butcher. Your meal will have the best flavor and nutritional value. We are sure you will love this Carnivore version of the classic Italian dish!

1 lb (455 g) fresh grass-fed beef tenderloin

¼ cup (56 g) Golden Marrow Fat (see page 143), divided

2 tsp (12 g) Smoked Salt (see page 136), divided

Freeze the tenderloin for 2 hours to firm up the meat for slicing. Chill the four plates you will use to serve the carpaccio.

Remove the meat from the freezer. With a very sharp chef's knife, cut it into ⅛-inch (4-mm) slices. Lay a piece of plastic wrap on your counter and place the slices, one layer thick, on the wrap. Cover the meat with another layer of plastic wrap. Very gently pound the meat with the flat end of a meat mallet until it's paper thin.

Warm the fat in a small saucepan until it is hot but not smoking. Divide the meat among the chilled plates. Sprinkle ½ teaspoon of the salt and 1 tablespoon (14 g) of the fat on each serving of meat. Serve immediately.

Nutrition Notes

An important benefit of eating raw meat is that it preserves the vitamin B6 content. B6 is easily damaged by heat and would not hold up to cooking. Including raw meat in your Purist Style diet will ensure you do not incur a B6 deficiency.

Grilled Butterflied Leg of Lamb

PURIST STYLE

We love the flavor of grilled meat. Just meat, salt and fire! We think that our DNA recognizes that flavor as nutrient-dense sustenance, as we are so attracted to it. A butterflied leg of lamb is the perfect cut for grilling, as the outside develops a nice brown crust and the inside remains a tender, juicy medium-rare.

1 (5–6-lb [2.3–2.7-kg]) boneless leg of lamb, butterflied

1 tbsp (15 g) fine sea salt, plus more for serving

About 1 hour before you start cooking, remove the lamb from the refrigerator to bring it to room temperature. Place the lamb on a plate and sprinkle both sides evenly with the salt.

Preheat your gas grill by turning all burners to high. Sear the lamb, fat-side down, on the hottest part of the grill for 5 minutes, until it is nicely browned. Flip and sear the second side for 5 minutes, until it's browned. If flame-ups occur, control them by spraying them with water from a squirt bottle.

Reduce the heat to low, and cover the grill. Cook the leg for 35 to 40 minutes, until a meat thermometer inserted into the thickest part of the leg reads 135°F (57°C) for medium-rare. Depending on the thickness of the leg, it might need more or less time.

Remove the leg from the grill and place it on a cutting board with grooves, to catch the juices. Let the meat rest for 10 minutes. Cut the roast against the grain into ½-inch (12-mm) slices. Serve the meat on a platter, drizzled with its own juices, and a sprinkle of salt.

Nutrition Notes

Lamb is an excellent source of protein and vital nutrients like iron, zinc, selenium and vitamin B12. A significant portion of lamb's wonderful fat is rich in anti-inflammatory, omega-3 fatty acids. In fact, most pieces of lamb contain even more omega-3s than beef!

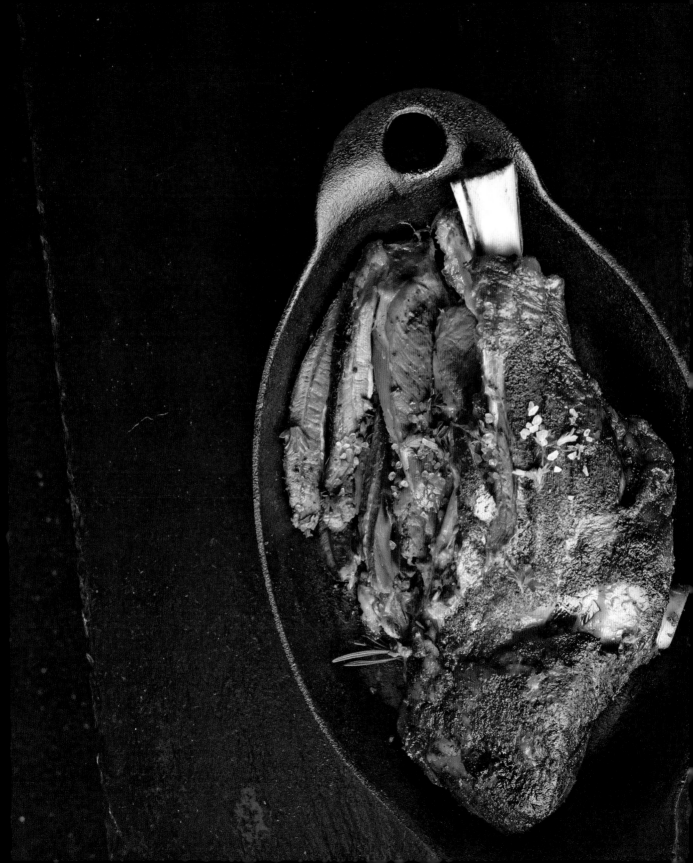

Easy Reverse-Seared Ribeye

PURIST STYLE

For us, ribeye is the king of all steaks, so it deserves special treatment. This reverse-searing procedure is worth the little extra effort to get a five-star, perfectly tender and juicy steak every time. In order to get the best results, you want the steak to be a minimum of 1½ inches (4 cm) thick. You can use this procedure even on a whole roast!

2 (1½-inch [4-cm])-thick ribeye steaks, about 1 lb (455 g) each

1 tsp fine sea salt

2 tbsp (24 g) tallow

Place the steaks on a plate, and season them on both sides with the salt. Let the steaks rest until they reach room temperature, about 20 minutes. Place a rack in the middle of the oven, and preheat it to 275°F (135°C). Arrange a small grilling rack in a baking dish.

Place the steaks on the rack, then bake the steaks, on the middle rack of the oven, for 15 minutes, or until a meat thermometer inserted into the thickest part of the steaks reaches 130°F (54°C) for medium-rare. The middle of the steak should appear slightly pink when it's cut into. Remove the steaks from the oven, and let them rest for 5 minutes.

In a large skillet, on the stovetop's highest setting, heat the tallow until it is fully melted. Sear the steaks, one at a time, for 1 minute per side, or until they are golden brown. Serve immediately.

Nutrition Notes

Ribeye is the greatest cut of meat for the Purist Style. Ribeye steaks provide about half the calories in fat, which is a perfect ratio for a healthy Carnivore diet. They also provide high levels of zinc and selenium, essential minerals to support your immune system and thyroid.

Per Serving:
Calories 320
Fat 14 g
Protein 46 g
Carbs 0 g

Smoky, Crusty, Tender Tri-Tip

PURIST STYLE

Tri-tip is a great, inexpensive cut of beef. If cooked right, this cut will give you the most delicious, tender, medium-rare bites combined with a nice brown outside crust. When you buy your tri-tip, choose a cut that's evenly marbled. The more marbling, the more flavorful the meat will be! It's very important to let the meat come to room temperature before cooking it.

1 tsp Smoked Salt (see page 136)

2 lb (910 g) grass-fed beef tri-tip, at room temperature

Rub the salt on all sides of the meat. Preheat your grill to high heat, then grill the tri-tip for 5 to 6 minutes per side, until a nice brown crust is formed on both sides.

Move the meat to indirect heat, or the side of the grill not directly over the flame, and cook it for 15 to 25 minutes, until a meat thermometer inserted into the thickest part reaches 130°F (54°C) for medium-rare. Because tri-tip varies so much in thickness from the tip to the middle, it is very hard to determine doneness by time alone; use the meat thermometer for best results.

Remove the meat from the grill, and let it rest for 10 minutes on a wooden cutting board. Cut the meat against the grain into 1-inch (2.5-cm)-thick pieces.

Nutrition Notes

Depending on the tri-tip you get, the fat content will range from 20 percent to 40 percent. We recommend adding extra fat to your plate when eating a recipe like this. The extra fat can be in the form of bone marrow, raw or rendered, or beef suet, quickly sautéed.

Grilled Sliced Brisket

PURIST STYLE

For best results, this brisket should be cooked on a cast iron grill placed over a real wood fire. It is important for the heat to be very high—around 500°F (260°C)—so the beef sears on the outside quickly, leaving the inside tender and pink. Also, the smokiness of the wood fire will impart a delicious aroma to the meat. In case that wood fire is not available to you, use your gas grill.

2 lb (910 g) brisket

Fine sea salt

Tallow, softened, for greasing the grill

To prepare the meat for slicing, freeze it for 8 hours, until it's solid in the center. Remove the brisket from the freezer, and let it stand at room temperature for 2 hours, until it's defrosted enough to slice.

With a very sharp chef's knife, cut the brisket into ⅛-inch (4-mm) slices. Lay the slices flat in a single layer on a cookie sheet, so they won't stick to each other, then sprinkle them lightly with the salt.

Brush some soft tallow on the grill so that the meat will not stick. You can cook the brisket directly over the fire, until it is charred on the outside but still pink inside, about 60 seconds per side for rare or 90 seconds for medium. Use a metal spatula to remove the brisket from the grill.

Serve immediately; sprinkle the beef with more salt, if needed.

Nutrition Notes

Brisket provides many B vitamins, including riboflavin, niacin, folate and pantothenic acid. It also provides 5.6 micrograms of vitamin B12, which helps promote energy and red blood cell health. Lean brisket is also a source of several minerals, including phosphorus, magnesium, potassium, zinc and selenium and 6.4 milligrams of iron per 8-ounce (230-g) piece.

Tongue and Marrow Broth Aspic

PURIST STYLE

Yields 8 servings
Per Serving:
Calories 460
Fat 32 g
Protein 37 g
Carbs 0 g

Aspic is such a retro recipe for most people. I, Vivica, grew up in Italy eating tongue in gelatin, and I have been trying to replicate that delicious flavor. I think we should make aspic cool again, as it is a very convenient way to preserve cooked meat and enjoy broth in the summer months.

1 tbsp (15 g) fine sea salt

1 whole grass-fed beef tongue

6 cups (1.4 L) Beef Bone Marrow Broth (see page 67)

6 tbsp (60 g) powdered beef gelatin

Nutrition Notes

This recipe is a great example of the nose-to-tail Purist Style of the Carnivore diet! Beef tongue is not only a great cut of fatty meat, it is also rich in fatty acids, as well as zinc, iron choline and vitamin B12. This meat is considered especially beneficial for those recovering from illness or for women who are pregnant.

In a large stockpot over high heat, bring to a boil 3 quarts (2.8 L) of water and the salt. When the water starts boiling, lower the heat to medium and cook the whole tongue for 1½ hours, until it starts getting soft when pierced with a fork. Remove the tongue from the water and let it rest for 20 minutes, until it is cool enough to handle. With a small and sharp knife, remove the skin from the tongue and trim any excess fat and glands from the bottom.

Place the cleaned tongue and the broth in an Instant Pot®, and cook on high pressure for 1½ hours, until the tongue meat is fall-apart tender. You can also cook the tongue and broth for 2 hours on low heat in a conventional pot, covered. You should end up with about 2 pounds (910 g) of tongue meat.

Cut the tongue meat into ½-inch (12-mm) slices and place them in a large bowl or dish of the shape you would like your aspic to be. Take a cup (240 ml) of hot broth from the pot and dissolve the gelatin in it, about 1 minute. Add the gelatin mixture to the rest of the broth in the pot, and whisk the mixture well to make sure the gelatin is evenly dissolved. Now, pour the broth over the meat, ensuring that all of the meat is submerged. Let the aspic cool at room temperature, then refrigerate it overnight.

To serve, soak the outside of the mold in a bowl of hot water for 1 minute, then invert it onto a plate. Cut the aspic into 1-inch (2.5-cm) slices.

Arrosticini: Italian Sheep Meat Skewers

PURIST STYLE

Arrosticini is regional Italian street food at its most delicious, and they're perfect for a person following the Carnivore diet! Two things give arrosticini their characteristic flavor: the type of meat and the style of cooking. The traditional meat used is a full-grown sheep, not lamb, so the meat is a bit tougher, but also very flavorful. If you can't find sheep meat, you can use lamb stew pieces or lamb neck meat. Try a cut with some marbling, as the fat adds flavor. The other secret ingredient is the wood fire. Arrosticini are cooked on real wood coals, which gives the meat its characteristic smoky flavor. If you can't use real wood, add some wood chips to the grill or the oven to replicate the flavor.

4 (12-inch [30.5-cm]) wooden or metal skewers

2 lb (910 g) sheep or lamb meat, cut into ½-inch (12-mm) cubes

1 tsp Herb-Infused Salt (see page 139)

If you are using wooden skewers, soak them in water for 1 hour before grilling. Thread the meat pieces onto the skewers, alternating fattier pieces with leaner pieces.

Prepare a grill over hot wood coals. Place the skewers over the highest heat, and cook them, turning every 2 minutes, until they are nicely browned on the outside and still pink inside, about 10 minutes total. Sprinkle with the salt. Serve the skewers immediately, and eat them with your hands!

Nutrition Notes

Lamb contains vitamin B12, which is essential for healthy nervous and digestive systems, for energy production and more. The selenium in lamb is a micronutrient vital for healthy cell division, protection from cancer, thyroid health and detoxification. Vitamin B3 in lamb is essential for the nervous system, helps the body make hormones and is important for healthy circulation. The zinc in lamb is a mineral with an important role in immune function, as well as the synthesis of proteins and DNA in the body. Lamb also has phosphorous, a mineral needed for healthy bones and teeth, as well as aiding the body in using carbohydrates and fats and making protein. Finally, the iron in lamb is a mineral that is necessary to make hemoglobin and myoglobin, the proteins in red blood cells and muscles that help transport and store oxygen.

Original Pemmican

PURIST STYLE

Yields 4 servings

Per Serving:
Calories 638
Fat 57.5 g
Protein 30 g
Carbs 0 g

What is pemmican? It's the original Carnivore meat and fat "bar," created by Native Americans as a nutrient-dense, calorie-dense, easy-to-transport, durable meal. Any lean cut of beef can be used for pemmican: bottom round, top round, eye of round, top sirloin and chuck shoulder steak, just to name a few. You could use tenderloin, but in our opinion, it is not worth the expense, as you will shred the meat after drying it. The leaner the meat, the easier it will be to grind into powder once dried. You can ask your butcher to slice the meat for you, which will make it much easier. This is the Purist Style version of pemmican; Berry Pemmican (see page 83) is an Ancestral Style version.

1 lb (455 g) lean grass-fed beef of choice (see headnote) cut into ⅛-inch (4-mm) slices

1 tsp fine sea salt

1 cup (198 g) homemade or store-bought tallow or Golden Marrow Fat (see page 143)

Smoked Salt (see page 136) or Herb-Infused Salt (see page 139), optional

You can use a dehydrator, if you have one, or you can use the oven for this recipe.

Lay the meat on the dehydrator racks and sprinkle it with the salt. Dry at 95°F (35°C) for about 12 hours, until the meat is dry and breaks instead of bending.

If you are using the oven, arrange a wire rack on a rimmed baking sheet, and lay the meat on the rack. Bake the meat at the oven's lowest possible temperature setting, 170 to 200°F (76 to 93°C), for 10 hours, leaving the oven door open a crack so steam can escape. Once the meat is dry—you will have about 7 ounces (198 g)—let it cool to room temperature.

Using a high-power blender, reduce the meat to powder. If your blender is not powerful enough, a coarse powder will work.

Nutrition Notes

Pemmican is the ultimate meal replacement or snack, as it provides perfect macros and great nutrient-density.

If you wish, weigh the meat, then measure the amount of tallow that equals the meat's weight. Place the powdered meat on a baking sheet. Heat the tallow for 5 minutes over medium heat, until it's melted. Carefully pour the tallow over the meat, and mix them together well.

Shape the mixture into bars or put it into silicone molds to get the shape you want. Let the pemmican cool completely. Sprinkle the top with the Smoked Salt, if using.

Pemmican can be stored in an airtight container at room temperature; it will last about a month unrefrigerated. If you refrigerate your pemmican, it will last up to 6 months.

Ribeye Steakon: Steak Bacon

PURIST STYLE

Yields 4 servings
Per Serving:
Calories 329
Fat 40 g
Protein 44 g
Carbs 0 g

I, Vivica, miss bacon sometimes! I stopped eating pork three years ago for spiritual reasons, and one of the things I miss the most is fatty, crispy bacon. So, a friend and I invented what we call "steakon" to use up the fatty steak pieces and make them feel like bacon. This recipe is also very similar to chicharrón, or fried pork skins. If you eat pork, use lard to fry the steak; it will make it even crispier and more like bacon! If you don't eat pork, this will really hit the spot. For this dish, make sure you use really fatty, well-marbled ribeye so that the meat will stay tender on the inside.

1 lb (455 g) ribeye steak, as fatty as possible, cut into 1-inch (2.5-cm) cubes

1 tsp Smoked Salt (see page 136)

½ cup (99 g) tallow or lard

Place the meat on a plate, and season it with the salt on both sides. Let the meat rest until it reaches room temperature, about 30 minutes. Line a plate with paper towels.

Heat the tallow in a cast iron or heavy-duty skillet over very high heat for 3 minutes, or until the tallow starts smoking. It's very important that the pan is very hot and the heat stays high to sear the outside of the steak while keeping the inside moist and tender.

Add the steak cubes to the pan, but don't overcrowd the pan. If the steak doesn't all fit in one layer, fry it in two batches. Fry the steak, stirring often, until the steak is evenly golden brown on all sides, 8 to 10 minutes. Drain the steak on the prepared plate, and serve the steakon immediately.

Nutrition Notes

Fat is really important in a Carnivore diet, especially when following the Purist Style. Ensuring you get the correct ratio of fat can make the difference between success or failure with the diet. For more details, please refer to the section on macros (see page 25).

Yields 4 servings
Per Serving:
Calories 510
Fat 41 g
Protein 30 g
Carbs 1 g

Pomegranate Grilled Lamb Chops

ANCESTRAL STYLE

There are three kinds of lamb chops that work well for grilling: loin chops, shoulder chops and rib chops. Just make sure that they are all cut to the same thickness as well as across the chop, so they will cook evenly. If you don't have an outdoor grill, you can cook this recipe on a grill pan or ridged cast iron skillet. The acids in the pomegranate juice will help make the lamb even more tender and digestible, especially when cooked medium-rare. The sugars in the juice will also give the meat a beautiful caramelized finish!

8 (1-inch [2.5-cm])-thick lamb chops

1 tbsp (15 g) fine sea salt, plus more to taste

2 cups (480 ml) fresh or bottled pomegranate juice

Place the lamb chops in a large, resealable plastic bag with the salt and pomegranate juice. Shake the bag well, so that the chops are coated evenly with the marinade. Marinate the meat in the fridge for at least 12 hours, or up to 24 hours, moving the bag a couple of times so that all the chops get to soak in the marinade.

Remove the lamb chops from the fridge at least 1 hour before cooking them, and let them come to room temperature. Drain the marinade from the meat and discard it.

Preheat a grill to high heat. Put a heatproof plate on the cold side of the grill. Grill the lamb chops for 3 minutes, then turn and grill the second side for 3 minutes, or until a meat thermometer inserted into the thickest part reaches 130°F (54°C) for medium-rare. Cook the chops for 3½ to 4 minutes per side, or to 150°F (65°C) for medium.

Place the chops on the warm plate, and let the meat rest for 10 minutes. Serve with a sprinkle of sea salt, if desired.

Nutrition Notes

This is a great higher-fat recipe, so you will not need to add much fat to the plate. Lamb chops have almost perfect macro ratios for a Carnivore diet.

Bacon Liver Meatballs

NUTRIENT-DENSE STYLE

Yields 4 servings
Per Serving:
Calories 702
Fat 49 g
Protein 55 g
Carbs 2.5 g

We used to call this recipe "offal for beginners," as the bacon really conceals the flavor of the liver, making it really easy to like, even for picky eaters. You can brine your liver overnight in the refrigerator in fresh whey, from raw milk, or in a mixture of ½ cup (120 ml) of water and 2 tablespoons (30 ml) of apple cider vinegar. It will help with the flavor and digestibility of the meat.

½ lb (230 g) fresh or frozen grass-fed beef liver

1½ lb (680 g) fresh or frozen grass-fed ground beef

½ lb (230 g) organic uncured bacon

2 organic eggs

1 tsp fine sea salt

If your meat is frozen, put it in the refrigerator at least 14 hours before you plan to cook it to defrost. When you're ready to cook, take the meat out of the fridge and bring the liver and ground beef to room temperature; this takes about 20 minutes. Line a plate with paper towels.

While the meat warms up, dice the bacon into ¼-inch (6-mm) pieces, then cook it in a cast iron or stainless steel skillet over low heat for 10 minutes, or until it's golden brown. With a slotted spoon, remove the bacon pieces from the skillet, leaving the fat in place, and place the bacon on the prepared plate to cool. In a food processor, mix the cooled bacon until it is reduced to crumbles.

Pat the liver dry with a paper towel and cut it into 1-inch (2.5-cm) chunks. Add the liver to the food processor, and mix until it forms a rough paste with the bacon. Add the ground beef, eggs and salt to the food processor, and pulse for 10 seconds, until all is well blended but not overblended. The mixture should have some texture, so make sure you stop mixing before it gets liquefied.

Form the meat mixture into 8 golf ball–sized meatballs, flattening them slightly. Heat the bacon drippings left in the skillet over high heat, then add the meatballs. Cook the meatballs for 2 minutes per side, until they are browned. Reduce the heat to low, and cook the meatballs, uncovered, for 10 minutes, until the meat is cooked but still pink inside.

Nutrition Notes

Liver is the true superfood of the Carnivore diet! In 100 grams of liver, you will find 53,400 IU of vitamin A. It is also a rich source of B vitamins and is the best source for the minerals copper and iron.

Fresh Liver Ceviche

ANCESTRAL STYLE

Yields 4 servings
Per Serving:
Calories 460
Fat 32 g
Protein 37 g
Carbs 0 g

Liver was a delicacy to our ancestors and it still is in many countries around the world! In Lebanon, you can eat raw lamb liver for breakfast, with a mint leaf and a sprinkle of cumin and salt. For this recipe, it's important to use the freshest, best-quality liver you can find. Grass-fed is a must here; it would be best to get your meat straight from your farmer. You can also experiment with lamb or goat liver; they are delicious in this recipe as well. The action of the acid in the lemon juice will "cook" the liver, giving it a briny, tangy flavor, very different from what one would expect from raw liver.

1 lb (455 g) fresh grass-fed beef liver

¼ tsp fine sea salt

Juice of 1 lemon

Freeze the liver for 20 minutes to get a firm consistency for slicing. Remove the liver from the freezer, and immediately slice it into ¼-inch (6-mm) slices, about 1 inch (2.5 cm) long.

Pat the liver slices dry with a paper towel, then place them in a bowl with the salt and lemon juice. Mix well and refrigerate the mixture for 30 minutes, or until the liver has turned uniformly pale. Serve cold or at room temperature, as desired.

Nutrition Notes

Liver is the ultimate ancestral superfood, so it is the perfect supplement for the Ancestral Style. Liver can make a Carnivore diet sustainable indefinitely because it provides so many necessary nutrients. In this recipe, we also leverage the benefits of eating fresh raw liver, with all the enzymes, proteins and vitamins unadulterated by heat.

Roasted Short Ribs

PURIST STYLE

Yields 3 servings
Per Serving:
Calories 930
Fat 62 g
Protein 87.3 g
Carbs 0 g

This simple yet satisfying meal is so easy to make it will quickly become a favorite staple dish. Since fattier pieces of meat are more calorically dense, they tend to be more satiating and keep you full for hours. Short ribs are also a fairly inexpensive cut of meat, so it won't break the bank if you want to make this recipe often. Since the meat is slow-cooked until it pulls right off the bone, this recipe reheats really nicely without getting overdone or tough, like some cuts when they are reheated. This is a perfect cut for advance meal prep.

5 lb (2.3 kg) bone-in short ribs

2 tbsp (24 g) tallow or marrow

1 tbsp (15 g) fine sea salt, plus more to taste

1½ cups (360 ml) water or beef stock

Preheat the oven to 300°F (149°C), then place the short ribs in a broiler-safe baking pan.

Cover the short ribs with the tallow, then rub the entire outside of the ribs with the salt. Pour the water into the bottom of the dish, then cover the dish with aluminum foil to keep in the moisture while baking; this will ensure the ribs stay tender and moist. Cook the short ribs for 3 hours, or until the meat pulls off the bone easily.

Change the oven temperature to high broil. Remove the foil, then broil the short ribs, uncovered, for 5 minutes, until the meat has a crisp crust. Let the meat rest for 10 minutes, then serve. Add a pinch of salt, if needed.

Nutrition Notes

This simple, calorically dense dish is high in omega-3 fatty acids and anti-inflammatory properties, which is helpful for overall inflammation reduction, gut health and joint health. This higher-fat dish will also help you maintain consistent energy levels for longer periods of time.

Smoked Beef Jerky

PURIST STYLE

Yields 6 servings

Per Serving:

Calories 659

Fat 45 g

Protein 58 g

Carbs 0 g

Typically, we recommend fattier pieces of meats to use during the Carnivore diet. But, for making jerky, the leaner cuts work a bit better. Also, if you plan to save some pieces for a future snack, hike or camping trip, the leaner pieces won't spoil as fast. This jerky will keep in the refrigerator for 7 to 10 days. When looking for cuts for jerky, ask your butcher for the freshest cuts of London broil, sirloin, flank steak or New York strip, as any of these make fabulous jerky.

4 lb (1.8 kg) grass-fed New York strip steak, sliced into ¼-inch (6-mm) strips

¼ cup (72 g) kosher salt

1 cup (240 ml) water

Nutrition Notes

The benefit of having easy, ready-to-eat snacks is that it reduces stress and prevents last-minute decisions on what to eat. High-quality, homemade jerky is a great way to keep you full during a busy day. Once cooked, it requires no reheating. Jerky is a high-protein trailside snack and is good for refueling after a hike.

In a large resealable plastic bag, shake the steak, salt and water together to coat the meat. Be sure to get as much of the air out of the bag as possible, then put it in the refrigerator for 1 hour.

If you are using a smoker, preheat your smoker and set the temperature to low, 150 to 175°F (65 to 79°C) if your smoker will go that low. Lay your meat on the grill with the pieces at least ½ inch (12 mm) apart. Cook the meat strips for 4 to 5 hours, until the jerky is tender and dry on the outside and pulls apart easily. Turn the meat strips over after 2 to 2½ hours of cooking. Transfer the jerky to a storage container, and let it cool for 30 minutes before refrigerating it.

If you are cooking your jerky in the oven, take the bottom rack out of the oven and cover it with foil. Return the rack to the bottom slot of the oven. Preheat the oven to your lowest temperature setting, 170 to 200°F (76 to 93°C).

Place a metal rack on top of a rimmed baking sheet, and place the strips of beef on top of the rack. Let the meat cook for 2½ to 3 hours, opening the oven door every hour or so for 5 minutes to let the moisture out. You will know your jerky is done and tender when the fat is no longer dripping off. Take the jerky out of the oven, and let it cool for 30 minutes before storing it in the fridge.

Jerky stays at its freshest stored refrigerated for 7 to 10 days.

Perfect Pulled Beef Roast

PURIST STYLE

Yields 4 servings
Per Serving:
Calories 865
Fat 67 g
Protein 58 g
Carbs 0 g

For this recipe, we chose to use the chuck roast cut, which is the highly active shoulder muscle of the cow. This cut has great marbling that slowly breaks down as it cooks, leaving the meat melt-in-your-mouth tender. Other cuts used for roasting are rib roast, eye of round, tenderloin, top round, London broil, top sirloin and rump roast. When ordering from your butcher, ask for high-quality, grass-fed beef for the highest nutritional density.

3 lb (1.4 kg) boneless grass-fed chuck roast

3 tbsp (54 g) kosher salt

3 tbsp (36 g) beef tallow

2 cups (480 ml) Beef Meat Broth (see page 140)

Preheat the oven to 275°F (135°C). Sprinkle the roast with the salt. In a large ovenproof pot or Dutch oven, heat the tallow over medium-high heat for 3 minutes, until it's melted. Add the roast to the pot, and brown each side of the roast for 2 minutes, until it has a golden-brown, crust-like layer. This process seals in the juices of the roast and will leave you with a more tender piece of meat.

Add the broth to the bottom of the pot, and transfer it to the oven. Cook the meat, uncovered, for 4 hours, until it pulls apart easily with a fork. Once the meat has finished cooking, turn the temperature in the oven up to high broil. Broil the meat for 5 minutes, until the meat has a crisp crust.

Pull the roast out of the oven, and let it rest for 10 minutes before serving. Letting your meat rest gives the fibers of the meat a chance to relax; your meat will be extra tender by taking this last step.

Nutrition Notes

Slow-roasted beef is easy to break down, aiding digestion and adding to gut health. Consume the extra stock and fat from cooking the roast, as they are rich with nutrients and contain high amounts of magnesium, phosphorus and omega-3.

Bison Sausage

PURIST STYLE

Yields 6 servings
Per Serving:
Calories 734
Fat 41 g
Protein 91 g
Carbs 1 g

Traditionally, sausage is made from fattier cuts of meat and spices. However, if you are able to obtain fresh, grass-fed, hormone-free meat, you can get away with very little seasoning and let the flavor of the meat shine through. Homemade sausage is easy to make, once you get the process down. You can ask your butcher to grind a high-fat cut for you or grind your own with a meat grinder.

3 lb (1.4 kg) high-fat ground bison

¼ cup (72 g) kosher salt

¼ cup (48 g) tallow or rendered bacon fat, plus more for cooking

1 (8-oz [230-g]) package natural sausage casings, rinsed thoroughly

In a large bowl, knead the bison, salt and tallow together until all ingredients are fully incorporated.

Cut off both ends of a plastic bottle 3 inches (7.5 cm) in diameter so the bottle measures 3 inches (7.5 cm) long. Stretch one of the sausage casings over the outside of the plastic bottle so the bottle can act as a funnel. Tie one end of the casing so you can pack the meat against the knot as you create your sausage. Push the bison mixture through the funnel, packing it tightly as you go; use a spoon to aid in this process. Once you reach the desired sausage size, pull the bottle out carefully and tie the sausage tightly at the other end, as closely to the meat as possible. Repeat the process to make 12 sausages. Refrigerate the sausages for 1 hour before cooking them. The sausages can be refrigerated in an airtight container for up to 4 days.

To cook the sausages, melt tallow in a skillet over medium-high heat; add the sausages. Cook them, turning so they brown evenly, for 9 minutes, until the sausage stiffens and the inside is slightly pink when cut into. Alternatively, grill your sausages over medium-high heat for 7 minutes, or, our personal favorite, smoke the sausages for 30 minutes at 220°F (104°C).

Nutrition Notes

Bison is leaner than beef, so cooking the bison sausage in tallow adds a robust flavor. Tallow is rendered fat originally used for cooking and frying. Like bison, tallow is rich in omega-3s, making this meal delicious and nourishing.

Beef Bone Marrow Broth

PURIST STYLE

Yields 5 servings
Per Serving:
Calories 464
Fat 35 g
Protein 34 g
Carbs 0 g

Nutrient-rich bone broth is a staple in the Carnivore diet. It's easy to make, and it adds flavor, nutritional density and variety to the cooking methods practiced in the Carnivore diet. Beef bone broth is not only savory and delicious, but also high in health-boosting properties. Bone broth can be made from just about any bones; even leftover bones make a great base for soups or many other recipes. The healthiest and richest-flavored broths are made from joints that contain cartilage and larger bones that contain marrow. When looking for bones for marrow broth, ask your butcher for grass-fed beef marrow bones for stew.

2 lb (910 g) grass-fed beef marrow bones

5 tbsp (74 g) fine sea salt, divided, plus more to taste

6 qt (5.7 L) filtered water

Preheat the oven to 450°F (232°C). Spread the bones, fat-side up, in a baking dish or pan. Sprinkle the bones with 2 tablespoons (30 g) of the salt and roast the marrow bones for 20 minutes. Pull the baking dish out of the oven and set it aside for 10 minutes to cool the bones.

In a large soup pot over medium-high heat, bring the water to a boil, and add the remaining 3 tablespoons (44 g) of salt. Add the bones and all of the drippings from the baking dish to the soup pot. Turn the heat to low, and simmer the broth for 90 minutes.

Remove the broth from the heat. When the broth and bones are cool enough to handle, clean the bones thoroughly and remove them from the broth. Make sure you scrape out any excess marrow and fat that may be inside of the bones; your soup's nutrition and flavor will come from this. Blend the broth in a blender or with an immersion blender if you desire a smoother texture. Add some salt to taste, if needed.

Nutrition Notes

Bone marrow broth has an abundance of minerals that help develop and support the immune system. When consumed regularly, bone broth can support bone density and heal damaged mucosal lining in the digestive tract. A healthy mucosal lining is a vital contributor to digestion and nutrition uptake.

Carnivore Waffles

NUTRIENT-DENSE STYLE

Yields 4 servings of
3 waffles each
Per Serving:
Calories 345
Fat 24 g
Protein 32 g
Carbs 0.5 g

We love this Carnivore batter; you will be delighted to see that the texture is almost exactly that of a grain-based waffle! The cool thing is that you can use different kinds of meat for slightly different results. Chicken will give you a smoother batter, closer to waffles made from grain; beef will give you a heartier waffle; and lamb will taste almost like breakfast sausage. We slather our waffles in ghee. If you are following the Ancestral Style, you can also top them with fresh berries and honey.

1 lb (455 g) ground chicken, lamb or grass-fed beef, at room temperature

6 organic eggs, separated and at room temperature

½ tsp fine sea salt

2 tbsp (28 g) ghee or Golden Marrow Fat (see page 143), plus ghee for serving

In a blender, blend the meat, egg yolks and salt on high speed for 1 minute, until it creates a smooth paste; the mixture should look a lot like pancake batter. Whisk the egg whites with an electric mixer until they start to form stiff peaks. You will need to scrape down the sides of the mixer with a rubber spatula several times. A stiff peak stands straight up when the beaters are lifted from the egg whites.

Gently incorporate the meat paste into the egg whites with the mixer on low, trying not to overmix. Overmixing after the egg whites have stiffened will cause the egg whites to lose their airiness.

With some of the ghee, grease the waffle maker on both sides and preheat it to medium-high. Pour ¼ to ⅓ cup (60 to 80 ml) of the batter on the waffle maker; depending on the size of the waffle maker, this measurement may change. Re-grease the waffle iron as needed. Cook the waffle for 4 to 5 minutes, until it is golden brown. Repeat to make 12 waffles; keep them warm while you finish using the batter. Serve the waffles with a dollop of warm ghee, if desired.

Nutrition Notes

The Nutrient-Dense Style is great for transitioning to the Carnivore diet. If you are having a hard time giving up conventional foods, recipes like this one will help you ease into the diet gently.

Moose Meatballs with Duck Fat

NUTRIENT-DENSE STYLE

Yields 4 servings
Per Serving:
Calories 355
Fat 13 g
Protein 51 g
Carbs 0 g

If you can obtain wild game meat, you will benefit immensely. Wild game animals are free range and are able to eat their natural diet. While some specialty stores may carry elk and venison, you'll have to either hunt your own moose or order online. If you can't get moose, feel free to use elk or venison in this recipe. We promise, moose will be worth the search.

2 lb (910 g) ground moose, elk or venison

3 tbsp (50 g) Smoked Salt (see page 136)

¼ cup (56 g) duck fat

1 organic egg

Preheat the oven to 350°F (177°C). In a large bowl, knead together the moose, salt, fat and egg, until everything is well incorporated.

Pack the meat tightly into 1½-inch (4-cm) balls with the palm of your hands, and place them on a rimmed baking sheet 2 inches (5 cm) apart.

Bake the meatballs for 15 minutes, until they feel like they have a little bit of give when you push into them but they don't fall apart easily. Turn the heat up to high broil. Broil the meatballs for 5 minutes, or until the fat on the outside of the meatballs forms a nice crust. This is a perfect technique for cooking a tender, juicy meatball.

Remove the meatballs from the oven, and let them sit for 5 minutes before serving them.

Nutrition Notes

Moose meat is extremely high in protein, about 22 grams per 100 grams of meat. It's also packed with potassium, niacin, selenium and zinc. These minerals help your body metabolize food to boost your immune system.

Lamb Shank with Apricot and Smoked Salt

ANCESTRAL STYLE

Yields 2 servings
Per Serving:
Calories 911
Fat 63 g
Protein 66 g
Carbs 20 g

This recipe is a spinoff of a classic roasted lamb shank. The shank is the cut of lamb taken from the lower section of either the front or hind legs. Although the shank is actually quite tough, the meat is naturally high in fat, so it breaks down to a perfectly tender, fall-off-the-bone delicacy when it is cooked slow and low. Ground lamb is fairly easy to find at your local grocery store, but you may need to call ahead to reserve a shank cut from your butcher.

2 lamb shanks

3 tbsp (42 g) ghee or marrow, divided

1½ tbsp (26 g) Smoked Salt (see page 136), divided

½ cup (120 ml) filtered water, divided

¼ cup (40 g) chopped dried apricots, divided

Put a rack in the middle of the oven and preheat it to 375°F (191°C). Rub each shank with half of the ghee, then sprinkle it with half of the salt.

Tear off two arm-length pieces of foil and fold each in half. Place one shank in the middle of each piece of foil, and fold in the edges of the foil to make a bowl shape; this helps keep the liquid around the shank. Add ¼ cup (60 ml) of the water to each foil bowl, and sprinkle half of the apricots on the lamb in each of the bowls.

Place the foil bowls in a roasting pan, and tightly cover the shanks with the rest of the foil. Cook the lamb in the middle of the oven for 3 to 3½ hours, or until the meat is tender and pulls off the bone easily. Increase the temperature to high broil. Uncover the shanks, and broil them for 5 minutes, or until the meat has a crisp crust. Let the shanks rest for 5 minutes before serving them.

Nutrition Notes

Lamb shanks are so easy to cook, and they are packed with nutrition. Lamb is a great source of iron and calcium, which helps fight fatigue by producing and oxygenating red blood cells. Zinc is also found in lamb; the combination of zinc and iron can help boost your immune system, so take advantage of eating lamb during the cold season. The dried apricots in this dish provide a small amount of carbohydrates and fiber, along with an adequate amount of vitamin A, which helps maintain healthy skin, teeth, bones and soft tissue, as well as a healthy immune and reproductive system.

Filet, Marrow and Eggs

NUTRIENT-DENSE STYLE

Yields 2 servings
Per Serving:
Calories 841
Fat 62 g
Protein 71 g
Carbs 1 g

We have put this meal together to celebrate variation in textures and flavors within the Nutrient-Dense Style of the Carnivore diet. The crispy bone marrow and filet is a delicious meal in itself; the eggs just add to the pure decadence. Beef marrow bones are easy to find in most grocery stores; often they are labeled soup bones. If possible, use organic eggs. The taste is noticeably better and the nutrition profile is worth the extra cost.

2 grass-fed beef marrow bones, halved

4½ tsp (23 g) fine sea salt, divided, plus more to taste

2 (½-lb [230-g]) filet mignon steaks

6 organic eggs

Preheat the oven to 400°F (204°C). Place the bones on a large rimmed baking sheet, fat-side up, and sprinkle 1 teaspoon of the salt over the top of each bone. Adding the salt prior to baking helps the marrow crisp in the oven.

Bake the bones for 25 to 30 minutes, until the marrow is crispy on the outside and soft on the inside. Remove the bones from the oven and set them aside.

While the marrow bones are baking, preheat the grill to 400°F (204°C). Sprinkle the remaining ½ teaspoon of the salt on the steaks. Grill the steaks for 6 minutes on each side, or until a food thermometer inserted into the thickest part of the steak reaches 140°F (60°C). Avoid the hottest spots on the grill for this cut of meat to prevent overcooking; the hot spots are where the flames will come the highest or closest to where you placed your food. Remove the steaks from the grill and let them rest for 5 minutes.

Cook the eggs while the steaks rest. Spoon some of the excess marrow fat in the pan with the bones into a frying pan. Melt the marrow over medium heat, then crack the eggs and add them to the pan. Cook the eggs for 3 minutes, flipping once, for over-medium, or less or more time to your liking.

To serve, divide the marrow bones, filets and eggs between two plates. Salt to taste.

Nutrition Notes

With its extremely high nutrient density, this meal will fuel and satiate you for hours. The ingredients in this meal are full of collagen for gut- and tendon-healing, as well as high in omega-3 fatty acids. This is a great meal for fueling your day or to consume after a long day of fasting.

Roasted Beef Ribs with Coffee Rub

ANCESTRAL STYLE

Yields 4 servings

Per Serving:
Calories 1,009
Fat 89 g
Protein 36 g
Carbs 9 g

There are two kinds of beef ribs: full slab and short ribs. Full slab works best for this cooking method: grilling or baking in the oven on low; while short ribs work best for braising and slow cooking. The secret to fall-off-the-bone beef ribs is the slow cooking process and low oven temperature. Beef ribs aren't as available as pork ribs, but your butcher will be able to order them for you. Also, if you're buying ribs from the butcher, ask if they can remove the silver-skin membrane from the back for you.

2 slabs (2 lb [910 g]) grass-fed beef ribs, silver skin removed

⅓ cup (70 g) ghee or beef marrow

2 tbsp (30 ml) honey

3 tbsp (54 g) kosher salt

2 tbsp (10 g) coarsely ground coffee beans

Preheat the oven to 275°F (135°C). Line two rimmed baking sheets with foil.

Rub both racks of the ribs with the ghee, then the honey, salt and coffee. Place one rack of ribs on each lined baking sheet, then cover both racks with foil and put them in the oven.

Bake the ribs for about 3 hours, until the internal temperature is 200°F (93°C). Pull the ribs out of the oven and let them rest, uncovered, for 30 minutes to let out some of the moisture. Bake the ribs, uncovered, for 1 hour. The meat should easily pull off the bone with a fork; if it doesn't, cover the ribs with foil and bake them for 25 minutes longer, until the meat is tender and pulls off the bone easily.

Let the ribs rest for 10 minutes before serving them.

Nutrition Notes

Beef ribs are high in vitamin B12, which is necessary for the creation, maintenance and repair of red blood cells. B12 also promotes healthy hormone levels and mental well-being. Beef ribs also have zinc, which is essential for your immune system and brain function. The coffee grinds and honey add a different flavor, and the small amount of caffeine in the coffee grinds and carbohydrates in the honey make for a great evening meal after an active day.

Honey-Glazed Beef Spareribs

ANCESTRAL STYLE

Yields 2 servings
Per Serving:
Calories 802
Fat 54 g
Protein 69 g
Carbs 9 g

Looking for sweet, salty, buttery flavor and meat that falls off the bone? You are in the right place with this easy but mouthwatering recipe. This recipe is a good way to break up the monotony of just eating meat and salt and helps you add more carbohydrates to your Carnivore diet.

3 lb (1.4 kg) grass-fed beef spareribs

4 tsp (18 g) ghee, melted

2 tbsp (30 ml) honey

1 tbsp (17 g) Smoked Salt (see page 136)

Preheat the oven to 250°F (121°C). Place the ribs in a large baking dish, and let the meat come to room temperature, about 20 minutes.

Mix the ghee, honey and salt in a medium bowl. With a pastry brush, brush the ribs evenly with the ghee mixture. Cover the baking dish with aluminum foil, making sure the foil is as airtight as possible.

Bake the ribs for 4 hours without uncovering the dish. After 4 hours, remove the foil and place the ribs under the broiler on high for 5 minutes, or until the meat is slightly crisped and browned on top. Spoon some of the cooking juices over the ribs before serving them.

Nutrition Notes

This Ancestral recipe, because of the high sugar and fat content, could be great for athletes practicing a carb refeed but also needing more long-term energy and a high-calorie meal.

Succulent Skirt Steak

PURIST STYLE

Yields 4 servings
Per Serving:
Calories 460
Fat 32 g
Protein 37 g
Carbs 0 g

Skirt steak is one of our favorite cuts of steak! It's less expensive and super easy to make without any fancy equipment or techniques, not even a meat thermometer. You can cook skirt steak on the grill, as in this recipe, or on the stove in a cast iron pan. Skirt steak is not very fatty, so it's fun to cook it with different fats to add flavor and nutrition. Just make sure you don't overcook it; you want it to stay tender and succulent.

2 lb (910 g) grass-fed skirt steak, cut into 5-inch (12-cm) segments

1 tsp fine sea salt

1 tbsp (14 g) Golden Marrow Fat (see page 143) or fat of choice

Smoked Salt (see page 136) or Herb-Infused Salt (see page 139)

Pat the steak segments dry with a paper towel, then sprinkle them with the sea salt on both sides. Let the steaks rest and come to room temperature, about 15 minutes.

While the steaks rest, preheat the grill to high, and put a heatproof plate on the cold side of the grill to warm up. Grill the steak for 2 to 3 minutes, or until the meat is nicely browned. Flip the steak and grill it for 1 or 2 minutes, until the second side is browned.

Place the steaks on the warmed plate to rest for 3 minutes. Slice the steak against the grain into 1-inch (2.5-cm) strips. For serving, top the steak with the fat and the salt.

Nutrition Notes

The Purist Style is the ultimate elimination diet—allowing only meat, salt and water—so it is most suitable for people who need to heal from autoimmune or gastrointestinal disorders. The detoxification this powerful, clean diet provides also helps people with conditions like autism, Parkinson's and Alzheimer's.

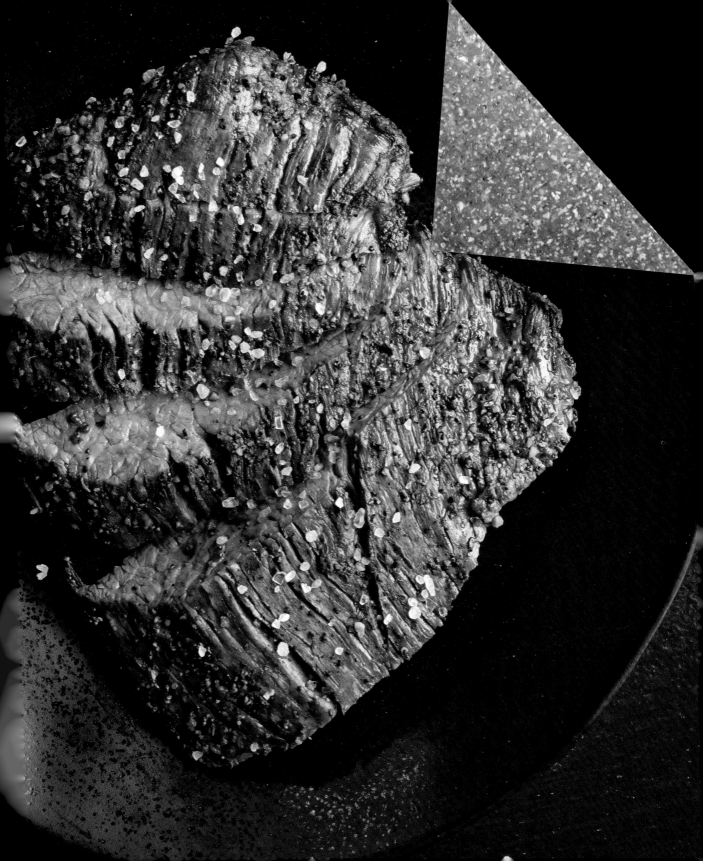

Berry Pemmican

ANCESTRAL STYLE

Berry pemmican is a delicious variation from the original one and makes a great kid-friendly snack. The berries also add some vitamins C, K and E.

Yields 4 servings

Per Serving:
Calories 669
Fat 57.5 g
Protein 30 g
Carbs 8.2 g

1 lb (455 g) lean meat of choice (see page 48), cut into ⅛-inch (4-mm) slices

1 tsp fine sea salt

1 cup (120 g) unsweetened dried blueberries

1 cup (140 g) unsweetened dried cranberries

1 cup (198 g) tallow or Golden Marrow Fat (see page 143)

Smoked Salt (see page 136) or Herb-Infused Salt (see page 139), optional

Nutrition Notes

The Ancestral Style of the Carnivore diet includes some carbohydrates, which can be beneficial for women with hormonal issues and athletes. Pemmican is the ultimate meal replacement or snack, as it provides a good amount of fat. It's very important to balance the protein-heavy meats with enough fat. Please refer to page 25 for more info about the best Carnivore diet macros.

You can use a dehydrator, if you have one, or you can use the oven for this recipe.

Lay the meat on the dehydrator racks and sprinkle it with the salt. Dry at 95°F (35°C) for about 12 hours, until the meat is dry and breaks instead of bending.

If you are using the oven, put a wire rack on a rimmed baking sheet and place the meat on the rack. Bake it for about 10 hours at the lowest possible setting, 170 to 200°F (76 to 93°C), leaving the oven door open a crack, so steam can escape.

Once the meat is dry—you will have about 7 ounces (200 g)—let it cool to room temperature.

Using a high-power blender, reduce the meat to powder. If your blender is not powerful enough, a coarse powder will work, too. Add the blueberries and cranberries to the blender, and blend until they are also powdered and mixed well with the meat.

Place the powdered meat on a rimmed baking sheet. Heat the tallow over medium heat on the stove for 5 minutes, until it's melted. Carefully pour the tallow over the meat mixture, and stir until it's well blended with the meat.

Shape the mixture into bars or put it in a silicone mold to get the shape you want. Let the pemmican cool completely. Sprinkle the top with the Smoked Salt, if using.

Pemmican can be stored in an airtight container at room temperature for up to 1 month or refrigerated for up to 6 months.

Honey-Orange Pulled Wild Boar

ANCESTRAL STYLE

Yields 5 servings

Per Serving:
Calories 633
Fat 21 g
Protein 77 g
Carbs 34 g

We have altered a favorite recipe to fit this Carnivore style, so you can now feast like your primal ancestors! While wild boar can be tricky to get at your local butcher, there are quite a few places online that offer a variety of the meat. Boar is similar to pork, but slightly darker due to its high iron content. Boar's texture is between pork and beef; it's lean and clean-tasting and can be used in any pork recipe. Because boar is usually not factory-farmed, it is naturally hormone and antibiotic free. For this tender, fall-off-the-bone, juicy recipe, we recommend either a boar shoulder roast or a rump roast. If you are dying to try this recipe ASAP, you can easily swap the boar out for pork shoulder or rump roast.

¼ cup (56 g) ghee or duck fat

4 lb (1.8 kg) wild boar shoulder or rump roast

3 tbsp (45 g) fine sea salt, plus more to taste

1 cup (240 ml) freshly squeezed orange juice

3 tbsp (45 ml) honey

5 oranges, unpeeled and cut in half, divided

½ cup (120 ml) filtered water

Preheat the oven to 225°F (107°C).

In a large ovenproof pot or Dutch oven, melt the ghee over medium-high heat on the stove. Sprinkle the boar with the salt, then cook each side of the roast for 90 seconds, or until browned. This step seals in the juices of the roast and makes for a juicier piece of meat.

Remove the pot from the heat and add the orange juice, honey, half of the oranges and the water. Cover the pot with a lid or foil. Roast the meat for 5 hours and 30 minutes, until it easily falls apart.

Increase the oven temperature to 400°F (204°C). Shred the meat with a fork and squeeze the juice from the remaining oranges over the meat. Roast the meat uncovered for 20 minutes, or until it has a glazed, crisp crust. Remove the orange rinds from the meat and discard them. Salt the meat to taste.

Nutrition Notes

Wild boar is much leaner than conventionally raised pork. It's also high in protein and low in saturated fat. The carbohydrates in this recipe make for a perfect recovery meal after exercise and physical activity. Because the roast breaks down as it slowly cooks, it's very easy to digest.

Cranberry Venison Jerky

ANCESTRAL STYLE

Venison refers to the meat of deer. It is a big game red meat that can be found in some specialty stores or easily ordered from your butcher. Venison has become increasingly popular due to its nutritional value. It's also more environmentally sustainable to eat than factory-farmed red meat. Since venison is already a very lean meat, almost any cut from the animal will work for jerky.

Juice of 1 orange

¼ cup (35 g) unsweetened dried cranberries

1 tbsp (15 ml) honey

¼ cup (60 ml) organic cranberry juice

2 lb (910 g) venison, cut into ½-inch (12-mm) strips

2 tbsp (30 g) fine sea salt

In a blender or food processor, blend the orange juice, cranberries, honey and cranberry juice until the ingredients are well combined, about 90 seconds. In a large bowl, combine the venison strips, salt and cranberry mixture; cover the bowl and refrigerate it for 3 hours.

Preheat the oven to 225°F (107°C).

Place a wire rack on top of a rimmed baking sheet, and place the venison strips on top of the rack 1 inch (2.5 cm) apart. Bake until the meat strips stop dripping fat and the jerky pulls apart easily; this will take about 3 hours. Turn the jerky over about 90 minutes into the baking time.

Fully cool the jerky—this takes 30 minutes—before storing it. Refrigerate the jerky in a glass mason jar or glass container for up to 7 days.

Nutrition Notes

Homemade venison jerky is packed with nutrition. The high protein content makes for a satiating snack. Venison is very lean but contains high amounts of omega-3s and vitamins B12, B6 and B3. The mineral content is also high in venison, which aids immensely while on a Carnivore diet. Zinc, selenium, phosphorus and iron are prevalent in venison. This recipe makes a great snack.

Yields 3 servings

Per Serving:
Calories 1,462
Fat 134 g
Protein 34 g
Carbs 30 g

Grilled Pork Belly with Dates and Eggs

ANCESTRAL STYLE

This recipe was put together in honor of brunch culture! Pork belly is the thick, fatty, boneless cut of meat from the belly of a pig. This is the piece of meat from which bacon is cut. Pork belly is uncured and unsmoked and can be prepared many ways, other than as bacon. When this cut is prepared correctly, it's tender and melts in your mouth. While this dish is considered a special occasion meal, it will quickly become a favorite.

1½ lb (680 g) fresh pork belly, skin removed and cut into 2-inch (5-cm) cubes

1 tbsp (15 g) fine sea salt, plus more to taste

5 dried Medjool dates, pitted and chopped

1 tbsp (14 g) ghee

6 organic eggs

Preheat the oven to 400°F (204°C).

Place the pork belly in a large bowl, and stir in the salt and dates.

Arrange the pork belly mixture on a rimmed baking sheet, being careful not to overlap the pork. Bake the pork belly for 30 minutes, then turn the pieces over gently and bake them for 20 to 25 minutes, or until they're crispy and golden brown.

About 5 minutes before you pull the pork belly out of the oven, heat the ghee in a large frying pan over medium-high heat on the stove for 1 to 2 minutes, until the ghee is fully melted. Crack the eggs into the pan and fry them, flipping each egg one time. We recommend a soft-cooked yolk, which will take about 2 minutes per side.

Serve the eggs over the pork and dates. You may need to salt the pork and eggs before serving.

Nutrition Notes

This recipe is high in fat, with a fair amount of carbohydrates, which means it will satisfy your hunger for a long period of time. Dates are high in natural sugars and fiber, making this meal perfect for pre- or post-exercise.

Coffee-Rubbed Roasted Venison

ANCESTRAL STYLE

Roasted venison is a delicacy if it is cooked correctly. The main mistake people make when cooking deer meat is overcooking, which makes the lean wild game meat rubbery rather than delicate and tender. In this recipe, we use the loin, which is the very tender cut just below the back-strap toward the rear end of the deer. Deer is quite versatile and can be used for stew, braising and roasting; it also makes great jerky.

½ venison loin (about 2 lb [910 g])

⅓ cup (27 g) premium coffee grounds

3 tbsp (45 g) fine sea salt

3 tbsp (42 g) ghee or tallow

Preheat the oven to 350°F (177°C). Rub the venison roast with the coffee and salt. In a cast iron skillet or ovenproof roasting dish, cook the ghee over medium-high heat for 2 minutes, or until it's melted. Sear the venison roast in the ghee for 2 minutes per side, until browned, to seal in the juices.

Roast the meat for 5 minutes per pound of meat, or until the internal temperature reaches 125°F (51°C) for medium-rare. Remove the roast from the oven, and let it rest for 5 minutes before cutting and serving it.

Nutrition Notes

Venison and other wild game meat are so beneficial to consume because the animal has the opportunity to eat its natural, wild diet. Venison is very lean and contains high amounts of protein, along with vitamins B6 and B12 and omega-3 fatty acids. Wild game is naturally lower in sodium, so you can add more salt to taste.

Smoked Prime Rib

PURIST STYLE

Yields 6 servings
Per Serving:
Calories 1,043
Fat 69 g
Protein 97 g
Carbs 0 g

Prime rib is a cut from the upper rib section of the steer, and it's one of the more sought-after large cuts of beef. The prime rib is beautifully marbled with fat, leaving this cut juicy and tender. When ordering the prime cut from your butcher, make sure you request an evenly marbled, high-quality, hormone-free piece. It will be worth every bite.

5 lb (2.3 kg) bone-in, grass-fed prime rib roast

3 tbsp (54 g) kosher salt, plus more to taste

2 tbsp (28 g) rendered pork or beef lard or tallow

Bring the meat to room temperature; this takes 1 hour.

Rub the entire roast with the salt. Melt the rendered fat in a large pan over medium-high heat. Sear the roast for 2 minutes per side to brown it and seal in the moisture and juices.

Set your smoker to 400°F (204°C), and let it preheat for 15 minutes. Place the roast on the grill, fat-side up. Reduce the temperature to medium-high (300°F [149°C]), and roast the rib for 35 minutes, then turn down the smoker to 250°F (121°C) and smoke the meat for 4 hours, or until the internal temperature reaches 125°F (52°C) for rare or 130°F (54°C) for medium-rare.

Remove the roast from the smoker, and let it rest for 10 to 15 minutes before slicing it. Add salt as needed.

Nutrition Notes

Because this is a higher-fat cut, the roast is very flavorful and satiating. Obtaining high-quality cuts will add to the clean flavor of meat, smoke and salt. The rib roast is high in vitamins B12 and B6, which boosts the immune system and protects against cancer and heart disease.

Ribeye Bulgogi

ANCESTRAL STYLE

Yields 2 servings
Per Serving:
Calories 679
Fat 31 g
Protein 75 g
Carbs 25 g

Bulgogi is a traditional Korean staple made with soy, sugar, vinegar and sesame, but in this version, you will find alternative ingredients, such as salt, honey and lime. All the ingredients listed in this recipe are easy to find. We suggest a boneless ribeye of bison or beef for easy cutting, since the meat needs to be cut thin, about ½ inch (12 mm) in thickness.

2 tbsp (30 ml) filtered water

2 tbsp (30 g) fine sea salt, divided

2 tbsp (30 ml) honey

½ cup (120 ml) freshly squeezed orange juice

1½ lb (680 g) grass-fed beef or bison ribeye, cut into ½-inch (12-mm) slices

2 tbsp (30 ml) freshly squeezed lime juice

3 tbsp (42 g) ghee or tallow

2 slices of fresh lime, for garnish

In a large bowl, mix the water, 1 tablespoon (15 g) of the salt, the honey and the orange juice. Add the ribeye, and toss it to coat the meat with the mixture. Stir in the lime juice. Cover and let the meat marinate for 2 hours in the refrigerator.

Heat the ghee in a large skillet over medium-high heat for 2 minutes, until it is melted. Pull the meat out of the bowl and place it in the pan. Pan-fry the meat for 6 to 8 minutes. The trick is to turn the steak strips as little as possible, so each piece gets a nice, golden-brown coating from the ghee. To test if the meat is done, cut one piece in half; if it is slightly pink on the inside, the meat is cooked. The meat continues to cook once it's taken off the heat, so taking it off a minute or two early is fine.

Sprinkle the meat with the remaining 1 tablespoon (15 g) of the salt, top it with the lime slices and serve.

Nutrition Notes

The citrus is complementary to the fat of a ribeye, aids in digestion and breaks down the meat to make each bite tender and delicious. This recipe is high in protein, with an adequate amount of fat and a small amount of carbohydrates, making this meal a perfect choice before training or exercising.

Carnivore Pancakes with Berry Compote

ANCESTRAL STYLE

This recipe offers a sweet, delicious, vibrant change from your daily routine. The texture of these pancakes is amazingly fluffy and the smell will remind you of perfect weekend morning pancakes. This recipe is good for meal preps, as the cooked pancakes store well in the refrigerator to be rewarmed as snacks.

Yields 5 servings

Per Serving:
Calories 582
Fat 34 g
Protein 38 g
Carbs 16 g

2 tbsp (30 ml) water
⅓ cup (40 g) blackberries
1½ tbsp (22 ml) honey, divided
½ lb (230 g) ground grass-fed beef
6 organic eggs
1 tsp fine sea salt
3 tbsp (42 g) ghee, divided

Start by making the compote. In a small saucepan over medium-low heat, simmer the water, blackberries and ½ tablespoon (7 ml) of the honey until the berries are broken down, about 8 minutes. Set aside the compote.

In a blender, blend the beef, eggs, salt and remaining tablespoon (15 ml) of honey for about 2 minutes, until the consistency is like a smooth whipped batter.

In a medium-sized nonstick pan over medium-high heat, melt enough of the ghee to coat the pan; you will cook the pancakes in batches, using 1½ tablespoons (21 g) per batch for greasing.

Using ¼ cup (60 ml) of the batter per pancake, fill the pan with as many pancakes as it will hold. Cook the pancakes for 3 to 4 minutes, until the batter starts to curl up or stiffen on the edges and you see small bubbles in the batter. Flip the pancake, then cook the second side for 3 to 4 minutes, until the pancake is firm all the way through. Because the pancake is made from raw meat, it needs to be thoroughly cooked.

For serving, top the pancakes with the remaining 1½ tablespoons (21 g) of the ghee and the warm berry compote.

Nutrition Notes

Carnivore pancakes with berries were intended to break up the Carnivore diet's flavor profile and give you a treat. Differentiating tastes can often help keep you on the diet longer. Carnivore pancakes have a small amount of carbohydrates, so this recipe is great for post training or after a long hike.

LAKE
+ SEA

Baked Rainbow Trout with Orange and Thyme

ANCESTRAL STYLE

Yes, this recipe calls for thyme, but don't worry, you will not have to eat it. The thyme imparts flavor in the cooking and is then removed from the fish. In combination with the orange, it will create a subtle but distinct flavor signature.

1 tsp fine sea salt, divided

6 orange slices, divided

4 sprigs fresh thyme, divided

2 (12-oz [340-g]) fresh whole rainbow trout, rinsed and patted dry

2 tbsp (28 g) Golden Marrow Fat (see page 143), melted

Preheat the oven to 450°F (232°C). Line a large baking sheet with parchment paper.

Sprinkle ¼ teaspoon of the salt, then put 3 orange slices and 2 sprigs of thyme in the cavity of each fish. Close the cavity, brush the outside skin with the fat, then sprinkle ¼ teaspoon of the salt on the skin of each fish. Place the fish on the prepared baking sheet.

Roast the fish for 18 to 20 minutes, until the skin is crispy and brown and the flesh is fully opaque but still moist. To test for doneness, insert a knife along the backbone of the fish, at the thickest part, and pry the top fillet away from the bone; it should come away easily but still be moist nearest the bone.

Remove the thyme and oranges from the cavities of the trout, then transfer it to plates and serve it immediately.

Nutrition Notes

Rainbow trout is one of the best choices of seafood nowadays because of its low levels of contaminants, especially mercury. It is also rich in omega-3s, selenium, potassium and vitamins D and B12. Such nutrient-density makes it a great addition to your Ancestral Style of the Carnivore diet! For this recipe, we recommend using wild-caught fish, as farmed fish is often fed GMO grains and antibiotics.

Yields 4 servings

Per Serving:
Calories 143
Fat 4 g
Protein 14.2 g
Carbs 11 g

Pan-Fried Scallops with Papaya Noodles

ANCESTRAL STYLE

Scallops are mild, slightly sweet flavored and firm, like the texture of shrimp, instead of flaky, like cooked fish. For this recipe, use the big sea scallops instead of the smaller bay scallops. You can buy them fresh or frozen; let frozen scallops thaw in the refrigerator overnight. For best results, the scallops should be dried with a paper towel before they are seared and cooked in a large skillet to prevent overcrowding.

1 medium papaya, almost ripe but still firm

Juice of 1 lime

1½ tsp (7.5 ml) fish sauce, divided

1 tbsp (12 g) bacon fat or lard

1 lb (455 g) sea scallops, rinsed and patted dry

Peel the papaya skin with a sharp knife, then cut the papaya in half and remove the seeds. With a vegetable peeler, pare the papaya into noodles. Put the noodles in a bowl, and toss them with the lime juice and ½ teaspoon of the fish sauce. Divide the noodles among four serving plates.

Heat the fat in a large nonstick skillet over high heat, until it barely starts smoking. Place the scallops, generously spaced out, in the skillet. Cook undisturbed for 2 to 3 minutes, or until the bottom develops a golden crust. Turn the scallops and cook them for 2 minutes, then add the remaining teaspoon of fish sauce to the skillet. Cook the scallops for 1 minute, or until they reach an internal temperature of 120°F (49°C).

Serve the scallops hot over the papaya noodles, dividing any cooking fat remaining in the pan among the four plates.

Nutrition Notes

This is a delicious recipe especially suited for women in perimenopause or people with thyroid issues. Scallops are full of minerals and they are high in selenium, which is vital for thyroid health. Papaya is incredibly rich in enzymes and can help with constipation, which is a common issue with hypothyroidism. For those in perimenopause, it can be beneficial to add some carb cycling to your Carnivore diet, and the Ancestral Style is perfect for that. The macros of this recipe make it ideally suited for a carb-up!

Umami Scallops

NUTRIENT-DENSE STYLE

Yields 2 servings
Per Serving:
Calories 345
Fat 13.5 g
Protein 43 g
Carbs 5.5 g

For this recipe, you can either use the big sea scallops or the smaller bay ones. You can buy them fresh or frozen; let frozen scallops thaw in the refrigerator overnight. Shrimp powder and anchovy paste are not only extremely nutritious ingredients, but they also possess a strong umami flavor, which acts as a counterpoint to the mild scallops. You will be able to easily buy them online.

4 tbsp (56 g) ghee

1 tbsp (7 g) shrimp powder

1 tbsp (15 g) anchovy paste

1 lb (455 g) sea or bay scallops, rinsed and patted dry

Mix the ghee with the shrimp powder and anchovy paste until a smooth paste is formed. In a large nonstick skillet over medium heat, melt the ghee mixture and cook it for 1 minute, until it starts to brown.

Place the scallops in the skillet. Cook them, undisturbed, for 2 to 3 minutes, until the bottoms develop a golden crust. Turn the scallops and cook them for 2 minutes, or until they reach an internal temperature of 120°F (49°C). If you use bay scallops, start flipping them after an initial sear of 1 minute and cook them for a total of 3 to 4 minutes, until they are browned on both sides and fully opaque.

After removing the scallops from the pan, add 2 tablespoons (28 g) of ghee to the pan and deglaze it. Serve with the glaze on the side.

Nutrition Notes

The Nutrient-Dense Style of the Carnivore diet focuses on providing the most nutrition, so it can be sustained for long periods of time. Scallops are full of minerals, and they are high in selenium, which is vital for thyroid health. The anchovy, being an oily fish, is rich in omega-3 fatty acids, well-known for their ability to lower levels of triglycerides and cholesterol in the blood. It is also an excellent source of protein.

Yields 2 servings

Per Serving:
Calories 664
Fat 40 g
Protein 75 g
Carbs 1 g

Wild Boar–Wrapped Scallop Skewers

NUTRIENT-DENSE STYLE

For this recipe, we recommend using sea scallops. It's easier to wrap the wild boar around the larger scallops. The sweet flavor of the sea scallop with the salty wild boar bacon makes for the perfect mixture of sweet and salty. The succulent, juicy scallop, wrapped inside the crunchy, fatty bacon will make this recipe quickly become a favorite. We have mentioned boar can be tricky to find at your local grocery store, but you can order it online from a number of reputable farmers.

10 pieces wild boar bacon or medium-cut pork bacon

1 lb (455 g) sea scallops, rinsed and patted dry

2 tbsp (28 g) ghee or duck fat

Fine sea salt, to taste

In a large pan, cook the bacon on the stove over medium-low heat for 5 minutes. The bacon should be almost cooked but still pliable and easy to wrap and bend. Remove the excess bacon fat from the pan, and save it for another dish. Clean the pan and set it aside.

Wrap one piece of bacon around each scallop and secure the bacon with a toothpick or skewer. Melt the ghee in the pan over medium-low heat; add the wrapped scallops to the pan. Cook the scallops for 3 to 4 minutes on each side, or until they reach an internal temperature of 120°F (49°C).

Remove the scallops from the pan and let them rest for 5 minutes before serving them. Salt to taste.

Nutrition Notes

Scallops are one of the cleanest shellfish available. They do not filter water the same way clams and mussels do, so they are less susceptible to toxins and contaminants. Scallops offer a wide range of nutritional benefits, such as high omega-3 fatty acids, vitamin B12 and antioxidants, which are known to improve cardiovascular health. Since scallops contain large amounts of magnesium, this dish is great to ease and recover sore muscles.

Smoked Oyster and Cod Liver Pâté in Egg Cups

NUTRIENT-DENSE STYLE

This smoky, creamy, rich pâté will break up the monotony of simple foods! You can enjoy it by itself or as a side dish to any fish or seafood. It can be used as a sauce or, as here, as an appetizer, served in the boiled egg whites as cups. If you can't find oysters in water, you can use smoked oysters in oil, as long as you carefully drain off all the oil and pat them dry.

3 organic eggs

1 (3.75-oz [106-g]) can smoked oysters in water, drained

1 (4.3-oz [121-g]) can cod liver, drained

3 anchovy fillets

Bring a small pot of water to a boil, then add the eggs, in their shells, and boil them for 8 minutes, until they are almost hard-boiled. Cool the eggs, then peel them. Cut the eggs in half lengthwise and remove the yolks gently without breaking the whites.

In a small food processor, blend the egg yolks, oysters, liver and the anchovies. Blend for a minute or so, until the mixture is creamy. Fill the empty egg whites with the pâté, and place the cups in a glass storage container. Refrigerate the cups for at least 2 hours before serving them. The cups will last in the refrigerator for 4 to 5 days.

Nutrition Notes

This Nutrient-Dense recipe is not just a fat bomb, it's a nutrient bomb! When following the Carnivore diet, it is really important to be able to maintain that 70 percent fat ratio (see page 25), but it is not always easy to accomplish, even with eating fatty meats. This glorious pâté will provide plenty of fat and lots of good stable energy. It's a great recipe for endurance athletes, like runners and swimmers, and for anybody who is recovering from serious conditions.

Grilled Rock Oysters with Citrus Ghee

ANCESTRAL STYLE

Yields 4 servings
Per Serving:
Calories 290
Fat 25 g
Protein 15 g
Carbs 1 g

We created this recipe for those giant monster oysters that are almost impossible to shuck when raw. We think eating oysters raw with just their brine is the most delicious and nutritious way, but this is a good alternative for times when you can't easily shuck them or you can't deal with eating them raw. Grilling them with the ghee adds a delicious note of creamy fresh citrus.

3 tbsp (42 g) ghee, melted
Finely grated zest of ½ lemon
Finely grated zest of ½ orange
12 large fresh rock oysters

For the citrus ghee, mix the ghee with the lemon and orange zests. Chill the mixture in the refrigerator for at least an hour; chilling overnight allows the flavors to blend better.

Preheat the grill to high heat. Wash the oyster shells with a brush to remove any sand or mud from the crevices. Place the oysters on the hot grill and cook them for 2 to 3 minutes, until they start to open. Remove the oysters one at a time, open them and carefully remove the top shell; you might need a knife to separate the two parts of the shell.

Put the bottom half with the oyster meat back on the grill. Add a bit of the infused ghee to each oyster and cook them for 1 minute, until they start to bubble. Do not overcook; the oysters will become tough and rubbery. Serve immediately, being careful not to spill the cooking juices.

Nutrition Notes

This Ancestral Style recipe is great for women seeking to improve their fertility. Oysters contain a variety of important nutrients, and they're one of the traditional foods Polynesian South Sea Islanders used to make sure women would conceive healthy babies.

Lime Ceviche with Mango

ANCESTRAL STYLE

Yields 2 servings

Per Serving:
Calories 365
Fat 4 g
Protein 59 g
Carbs 19 g

We don't have to use heat to cook. Marinating fish in fresh lime juice adds a bright flavor; the acid from the lime juice helps "cook" the raw fish and firms up the texture. Pairing the fish with ripe mango and salt adds a nice balance to the bite of the citrus and makes for a light yet satiating meal. Fresh fish is key to making ceviche; ask for sashimi-grade fish when ordering from your fish market. You can substitute halibut or salmon, depending on what is in season, for the red snapper.

1 lb (455 g) sashimi-grade red snapper, skin removed, flesh cut into ½-inch (12-mm) pieces

1 tsp fine sea salt

¾ cup (180 ml) freshly squeezed lime juice

1 ripe mango, peeled and cut into ½-inch (12-mm) pieces

Place the fish in a large glass bowl. Add the salt and lime juice. The juice should fully cover the fish. Add the mango, and gently stir to coat the ingredients with the lime juice. Cover the bowl, and refrigerate it for 3 to 4 hours, or until the fish becomes opaque in color. Drain the fish and serve it immediately.

Nutrition Notes

Besides adding a vibrantly fresh, colorful dish to your routine, you will benefit from the small amount of complex carbohydrates in this dish. This easy-to-digest option is a great meal to add pre- or post-physical activity or for an extra boost of energy midday.

Branzino al Sale: Salt-Crusted Sea Bass

NUTRIENT-DENSE STYLE

Yields 1 serving
Per Serving:
Calories 545
Fat 33 g
Protein 60 g
Carbs 2 g

Salt-crusting is one of the oldest and healthiest methods of cooking. The salt aids in cooking the fish more evenly, while adding delicate flavor and locking in the moisture, to make the fish even more tender and flaky. Branzino is a fish caught off the coast of Italy and other Mediterranean countries. This fish has become more popular due to its flavorful, oily meat. You can order sea bass at your local fish market or from the butcher at your grocery store.

4 organic egg whites

2 lb (910 g) sea bass, rinsed and patted dry

2 cups (538 g) coarse sea salt or kosher salt

3 tbsp (42 g) ghee, melted

Preheat the oven to 400°F (204°C).

Beat the egg whites with an electric beater for 4 minutes, until the egg whites start to create stiff peaks. You will need to scrape down the sides of the mixer with a rubber spatula several times. A stiff peak stands straight up when the beaters are lifted from the egg whites. Cover the fish entirely with the egg whites, then, on a baking sheet, fold the salt around the fish so the fish is completely covered in salt. The salt should look like a coating held on with the egg whites.

Bake the fish, uncovered, in a baking dish or Dutch oven for 30 minutes, until the fish is white and flaky and the flesh pulls apart easily when tested with a fork. Remove the fish from the oven, and let it rest for 10 minutes. Break the salt away, and serve the fish with the ghee drizzled on top.

Nutrition Notes

Sea bass, like other white fish, is high in omega-3 fatty acids. Omega-3 balances out omega-6, which we consume too much of in our daily lives. Omega-3 helps fight inflammation, while helping the body's natural ability to heal injuries. Sea bass also has high amounts of vitamin D, which boosts your immune system and gives you energy while improving your mood.

Honey-Citrus Baked Salmon

ANCESTRAL STYLE

Yields 2 servings

Per Serving:
Calories 599
Fat 35 g
Protein 50 g
Carbs 21 g

Salmon is a freshwater and saltwater fish. It's extremely versatile to cook with, and, once you get the preparation down, you will be able to create recipes using this cooking style. This recipe is light, vibrant and super easy. The tangy citrus glaze pairs perfectly with the buttery, flaky salmon; this recipe is a great option on a summer day. Salmon is readily available at your fish market. For the best taste and nutritional value, make sure that you are buying wild-caught salmon.

1 lb (455 g) salmon fillet
Juice of 1 lime
Juice of 1 orange
Juice of 1 lemon
1½ tbsp (22 ml) honey
3 tbsp (42 g) ghee
1 tbsp (17 g) coarse sea salt or kosher salt

Preheat the oven to 400°F (204°C). Take the salmon out of the refrigerator and let it come to room temperature; this takes 15 minutes.

In a small saucepan over medium-low heat, simmer the lime, orange and lemon juices and the honey for 8 minutes, until the liquid starts to reduce and thicken. Add the ghee to the saucepan and whisk it in until all ingredients are combined. Take the saucepan off the heat, and set it aside.

Place the salmon on a metal baking sheet and sprinkle the salt evenly over it. Gently pour one-half of the glaze evenly over the salmon. Bump the temperature in the oven up to high broil, and put the salmon into the oven. Cook the fish for 14 minutes, until the internal temperature reaches 145°F (63°C). Keep in mind that every broiler is different; to avoid overcooking, check the salmon's internal temperature at the halfway point of the cooking time.

Remove the salmon from the oven, and cover it with the remaining citrus glaze. Let the salmon rest for 5 minutes before serving it.

Nutrition Notes

Most consider wild-caught salmon to be one of the healthiest foods. Consuming salmon on a semi-regular basis can strengthen the cardiac muscles and lower cholesterol, because the fish is rich in omega-3. This recipe is a perfect choice to fuel your body before or after exercise, because the citrus and honey provide a small amount of carbohydrates and it's an easy-to-digest protein.

FOWL

Smoked Turkey Legs

NUTRIENT-DENSE STYLE

Smoked turkey legs are a summer tradition. This favorite is lean, high in protein and great for barbecuing or throwing on your smoker. Turkey legs are easy to find year-round; for the best taste, make sure you are getting free range, antibiotic-free turkey legs.

Yields 3 servings

Per Serving:
Calories 918
Fat 54 g
Protein 108 g
Carbs 0 g

3 turkey legs (about 2½ lb [1.2 kg])

2 tbsp (28 g) ghee

2 tbsp (34 g) Smoked Salt (see page 136)

Preheat your grill to high, 425°F (218°C).

Slather your turkey legs with the ghee and cover them with the salt. Loosely wrap each leg in foil, and place the legs on the grill. Turn the grill down to medium heat, 400°F (204°C).

Cook the turkey legs on each side for 3 minutes, then move the legs to the top rack and cook them for 45 minutes, until the internal temperature of the turkey legs reads 165°F (74°C).

If you are smoking your turkey legs, set your smoker to 240°F (115°C), and smoke the legs for 2 hours and 30 minutes, or until the internal temperature reaches 165°F (74°C).

Nutrition Notes

Turkey and other white meats are naturally leaner, with a lower fat profile than red meat. Turkey meat contains lysine, tryptophan and vitamin B3, which is good for building the immune system, supporting thyroid health and maintaining healthy brain function. This recipe is lean enough to be the perfect post-workout recovery fuel.

Carnivore Breakfast Crepes

NUTRIENT-DENSE STYLE

Yields 4 servings
Per Serving:
Calories 169
Fat 9 g
Protein 20 g
Carbs 0 g

We were delighted and proud of ourselves to have created this recipe, which calls for boiled chicken meat, as it uses a leftover food that could otherwise go to waste. This recipe is the perfect companion to the Chicken Bone Broth (see page 132). We love chicken broth, but the meat sometimes can be too dry and bland to eat by itself, but we hate just throwing it out. You can serve these wonderful crepes by themselves. If you are following the Ancestral Style of the diet, you can top them with fresh berries.

½ lb (230 g) cooked chicken meat, about the equivalent of 3 drumsticks

3 organic eggs

¼ cup (60 ml) water

¼ tsp fine sea salt

Ghee or Golden Marrow Fat (see page 143), for greasing and serving

In a blender, process the chicken, eggs, water and salt on high speed until a smooth batter is formed; it should be a bit runnier than pancake batter.

Grease a nonstick pan with some ghee, and heat it over medium heat. When the ghee is hot, add ⅓ cup (80 ml) of the batter to the skillet. Spread the batter thinly on the skillet with the aid of a spatula. Cook the crepe for 2 to 3 minutes, until it's golden brown on the bottom. Flip the crepe and cook it for 2 minutes, until it's golden and firm. Repeat until the batter is used up; keep cooked crepes warm while you finish cooking.

Serve the crepes with ghee.

Nutrition Notes

Nutrient-Dense recipes like this one are great for the whole family, are more appealing to kids and provide good fats and protein necessary for growth.

Chicken Heart Skewers

NUTRIENT-DENSE STYLE

Yields 6 servings
Per Serving:
Calories 115
Fat 7 g
Protein 11 g
Carbs 0.5 g

Chicken hearts are a delicious treat in many cultures! They are an inexpensive way to get nutrients and high-quality protein, and, when prepared the right way, they are mouthwatering little bites. These make great appetizers. If you want to use the skewers for a main course, the yield is four servings.

6 (12-inch [30.5-cm]) wooden or metal skewers

1 lb (455 g) chicken hearts

1 tsp fine sea salt, divided

If you are using wooden skewers, soak them in water for 1 hour before grilling. Bring the chicken hearts to room temperature; this takes 30 minutes.

Clean the chicken hearts by rinsing them under cold water, then drain them well. Pat them dry with a paper towel. You can trim any veins or hard pieces from the tops of the hearts with a sharp knife. Thread the hearts onto the skewers, and sprinkle them with ½ teaspoon of the salt. Make sure the hearts are dry before you put them on the grill.

Heat the grill to 500°F (260°C). Grill the skewers over direct high heat for 8 to 10 minutes, depending on the size, until the hearts are browned on the outside but still pink inside. During cooking, turn the skewers every 2 minutes so the hearts cook evenly.

Serve the hearts immediately, sprinkled with the remaining ½ teaspoon of salt.

Nutrition Notes

This Nutrient-Dense recipe is great for everyone, as we consider organ meats to be one of the ultimate superfoods! Chicken hearts are a very good source of protein, the B vitamins—especially B12—riboflavin, zinc, selenium and iron. Chicken hearts also provide folate, magnesium, manganese, phosphorus, potassium, sodium and copper. Of course, the nutritional value of hearts from pasture-raised chickens will be vastly superior to those from chickens raised conventionally and fed pesticide-laden GMO corn and soy.

Bone Marrow and Chicken Liver Pâté

NUTRIENT-DENSE STYLE

Marrow and liver are the superfoods of this diet! Combining them creates one of the best nutrient-dense combinations you can imagine. This creamy pâté will also provide much of the fat needed in a protein-rich Carnivore diet.

Yields 8 servings

Per Serving:
Calories 290
Fat 26 g
Protein 11 g
Carbs 0 g

1 lb (455 g) organic chicken livers

½ lb (230 g) raw beef marrow

1 tsp Herb-Infused Salt (see page 139)

Bring the chicken livers and marrow to room temperature; this takes 1 hour. Drain any blood from the livers and pat them dry.

Warm a large nonstick skillet over high heat, then cook the marrow for 2 to 3 minutes, until it is mostly melted and brown. Add the livers to the skillet and sauté them for 3 minutes, until they are browned outside but still pink inside. Remove the skillet from the heat, and let the liver and marrow mix cool for 5 minutes.

Place the mixture in a food processor with the salt and blend until it's smooth. Pour the pâté into a glass storage container and refrigerate it for a minimum of 12 hours or up to 48 hours, so the flavors blend together.

Nutrition Notes

The Nutrient-Dense Style promises to deliver exactly that: nutrients! Liver is the superfood of the Carnivore diet. Because of the big vitamin B content, it will boost energy, while the vitamin A will help with healthy cell production and youthful skin. The presence of K2 helps calcium balance and brain health.

Crispy Eggs and Anchovies

NUTRIENT-DENSE STYLE

Yields 2 servings

Per Serving:

Calories 290

Fat 25 g

Protein 15 g

Carbs 1 g

Like a true Italian, I, Vivica, love anchovies: They have the ultimate umami flavor! What better umami marriage than a perfectly fried egg with a creamy, runny yolk? But wait, it gets better! Inspired by famous New York restaurateur Frank Prisinzano, who made the crispy egg a cultural phenomenon, I decided to marry my umami delight with a crispy egg and use what I call liquid gold to fry it in (Golden Marrow Fat [page 143]). Behold the results. You can substitute the same amount of ghee for this recipe for a flavor variation.

1 tbsp (14 g) Golden Marrow Fat (see page 143)

4 organic eggs

4 anchovy fillets

Pinch of fine sea salt, optional

Warm a stainless steel or cast iron skillet on high heat for 1 minute, then add the fat and let it heat for 30 seconds, until it barely starts smoking. Carefully add the eggs to the skillet, as the fat will splash and bubble. Lay the anchovy fillets gently across the yolks.

Lower the heat to medium-high. Cook the eggs for 1 minute and 30 seconds, or until the whites are fully opaque and the edges are brown and crispy. The yolk should be still runny. Sprinkle with a pinch of sea salt, if using, and serve immediately.

Nutrition Notes

This recipe is great for women with fertility issues and for people who lack nutrients. Anchovies offer a very low heavy-metal content combined with high nutrients. They are an excellent source of calcium, iron and zinc. Anchovies are an ideal source of vitamins A and D and, more importantly, a unique source of long-chain omega-3 fatty acids—polyunsaturated fatty acid—or PUFA, for short.

Roasted Hen with Wild Boar

NUTRIENT-DENSE STYLE

Yields 2 servings
Per Serving:
Calories 610
Fat 38 g
Protein 66 g
Carbs 1 g

Game hens are tender and succulent and resemble a small roasted chicken, making them great for a single serving. Game hens tend to be very lean, so adding wild boar to the recipe gives the meal extra fat and sustenance. You can find game hens in the meat department at your grocery store or at your local butcher. They are readily available year-round.

2 Cornish game hens, rinsed and patted dry

1½ tbsp (21 g) ghee or duck fat

1½ tbsp (26 g) coarse sea salt

8 pieces wild boar bacon or pork bacon

Preheat the oven to 350°F (177°C).

Rub the hens with the ghee and salt, then bake the hens in an ovenproof roasting dish for 30 minutes.

Take the hens out of the oven, and cover the top of them with the bacon. Bake the hens for 17 minutes, until the bacon is slightly crispy and the hen meat pulls apart easily with a fork.

Remove the hens from the oven, and let them rest for 5 minutes before serving them.

Nutrition Notes

Game hens have 24 grams of protein and less than 3 grams of fat per 3½ ounces (100 g) of meat, which makes them lean and high in protein. Pairing game hens with bacon or wild boar brings the caloric value up per serving to sustain you for longer periods of time than the chicken alone would. Game hens are high in vitamin B6, niacin and selenium.

Chicken Bone Broth

NUTRIENT-DENSE STYLE

Yields 3 servings
Per Serving:
Calories 160
Fat 16 g
Protein 4 g
Carbs 0 g

Bone broth is nourishing and delicious. We use bone broth as a flavorful base for soup and to add flavor while cooking. Bone broth is simple to make and easy to grab out of the refrigerator for a quick snack. We recommend buying a whole chicken and roasting it for a meal, then using the leftover meat and bones to make broth. Chicken bones are easy to find, but rarely sold as marrow bones, as beef bones are. You can make this recipe on the stove or in a slow cooker; the longer the broth simmers, the richer the flavor.

1 whole raw chicken or leftover roasted chicken

3 qt (2.8 L) filtered water

3 tbsp (51 g) Herb-Infused Salt (see page 139)

3 tbsp (42 g) ghee or duck fat

To make the broth on a stove, in a medium-large pot, combine the chicken, water, salt and ghee. Simmer the broth over low heat for 3 hours and 20 minutes, until the chicken meat falls from the bones.

To make the broth in a slow cooker, combine the chicken, water, salt and ghee. Cook the chicken on low for 4 hours, until the chicken meat falls from the bones.

Take the broth off the stove, and let it stand until it's cool enough to handle. Remove the meat and bones, and strain the broth with a sieve.

Nutrition Notes

The gelatin in bone broth is a vital nutrient for healing your gut and it also aids in joint health. Bone broth contains a large amount of collagen, which helps heal tendons, keeps hair and skin healthy and strengthens the immune system. Broth is easy to digest and is loaded with amino acids.

STAPLES
+ SNACKS

Smoked Salt

PURIST STYLE

Yields 2 cups (538 g)
Per Serving:
Calories 0
Fat 0 g
Protein 0 g
Carbs 0 g

Using a grill or smoker to flavor salt is a great way to add more depth and boldness to the recipes you're making while on the Carnivore diet. The process is simple, and you can smoke a large amount of salt at once and store it for later use. We use coarse sea salt, so there is more surface to soak up the smoky flavor, but you can also try kosher salt. This recipe calls for hickory smoking chips, but feel free to try different chips—apple, cherry or maple, for example—to acquire flavors you enjoy. You can purchase smoking chips at most grocery and hardware stores.

Hickory smoking chips

2 cups (538 g) coarse sea salt or kosher salt

Prepare your smoker for the lowest temperature, preferably under 80°F (26°C), but up to 150°F (66°C) will work if that is your smoker's lowest temperature. Place the hickory chips according to the instructions for your smoker.

Spread your salt over a metal baking pan, and place the pan in the smoker, uncovered, for at least 4 hours. Shake the baking pan every hour to rotate the salt.

Smoking salt for longer than 4 hours will continue to build a smoky flavor. You can smoke the salt for up to 12 hours.

Nutrition Notes

You can also put fresh herbs over the salt as you smoke it to infuse different flavors. Place sprigs of sage, thyme, rosemary or oregano over the salt. Pull the herbs out of the salt after 4 hours. Replace regular salt with smoked or infused salt in any recipe to add flavor and boldness.

Herb-Infused Salt

PURIST STYLE

Yields 2 cups (538 g)
Per Serving:
Calories 0
Fat 0 g
Protein 0 g
Carbs 0 g

Flavoring your salt is a great way to add depth and boldness to your foods. Coarse salt tends to work best for flavoring, as it has a larger surface area to absorb flavor. You can purchase or grow your own garden-fresh herbs for infusing salt. Fresh herbs work better. As the salt dries the herbs, the herbs excrete a light oil that flavors the salt. This process won't happen if you use dried herbs, because the oils are extracted by the drying process. For a bolder flavored salt, use fresh, organic herbs.

2 cups (538 g) coarse sea salt or kosher salt

8 sprigs fresh rosemary

Place the salt and rosemary in a mason jar or glass bowl, then cover the container. Shake or stir the mixture, and leave it, covered, in a dry place for 2 days. The longer the salt sits with the fresh herbs, the bolder the flavor will be.

Remove the rosemary before using the salt.

Nutrition Notes

Feel free to mix and blend your own herbs of choice to infuse your salt. Herb-infused salts last a very long time: up to 3 years, if you can keep the jar sealed and dry.

Beef Meat Broth

PURIST STYLE

Yields approximately
10 servings
Per Serving:
Calories 185
Fat 12 g
Protein 8 g
Carbs 0 g

This recipe is especially indicated for people who have a histamine intolerance. Unlike regular bone broth, meat broth is cooked for only 2 hours. To keep the histamines low, it's best to get the meat fresh from a butcher or from a supplier who guarantees that it was frozen immediately after processing. The best cuts of meat for meat broth are beef shank, beef brisket, oxtail, top sirloin and bottom round steak.

2 lb (910 g) mixed grass-fed meat
for broth (see headnote)

2 grass-fed beef marrow bones

1 tbsp (15 g) fine sea salt

3 qt (2.8 L) water

In a stockpot, bring the meat, bones, salt and water to a boil. When the water starts boiling, skim off the foam on top of it with a large spoon or ladle. Once you have removed all the foam, reduce the heat to low, and cook the broth for a total of 2 hours from the moment it started boiling.

When the broth is ready, remove the meat and bones, and pass the broth through a sieve. As soon as the broth reaches room temperature, it is important to pour it into silicone molds for freezing. Once the broth is frozen, you can transfer the cubes to resealable plastic freezer bags. The meat from the broth can be eaten with just a bit of salt.

Nutrition Notes

You will benefit most from this recipe if you have a histamine sensitivity, an autoimmune condition, a digestive disorder or any gastrointestinal issues. This broth can be used both for drinking and as a base for other recipes.

Golden Marrow Fat

PURIST STYLE

Yields 16 servings of
1 tablespoon (14 g)
Per Serving:
Calories 130
Fat 14 g
Protein 0 g
Carbs 0 g

4 lb (1.8 kg) grass-fed beef marrow bones, cut crosswise into 2–3-inch (5–7.5-cm) segments

Bone marrow is best known for being used to make broth, along with the whole bone. Not many people actually take advantage of the pure marrow fat. This is one of our favorite cooking fats: It's pure liquid gold! We love the flavor, as well as the high smoke point, and it's extremely easy and quick to make. You can't go wrong with marrow fat.

Preheat the oven to 300°F (149°C). Place the bones upright in a large, glass ovenproof dish. Bake the bones for 45 minutes, until the marrow is cooked and the fat, melted, collects in the bottom of the dish.

Remove the dish from the oven, remove the bones and carefully pour the melted fat into a mason jar. When the temperature is below 75°F (24°C) you can store the mason jars at room temperature. In warmer months, store them in the fridge.

You can use the bones for broth, adding them to fresh ones, as in the recipe for Beef Bone Marrow Broth (see page 67).

Nutrition Notes

Conjugated linoleic acid (CLA), a compound in bone marrow, has been found to reduce several markers of inflammation in the blood. Bone marrow also contains adiponectin, a type of protein hormone that has been shown to help regulate inflammation and immune function. Bone marrow also contains collagen, glycine and glucosamine.

Creamy Carnivore Fat Bomb

NUTRIENT-DENSE STYLE

Yields 2 servings
Per Serving:
Calories 282
Fat 39 g
Protein 2.5 g
Carbs 0 g

One of the issues with the Carnivore diet is that you may get too much protein and not enough fat. In the chapter about the Carnivore diet styles, we explain the ideal macros. We recommend giving it a peek (see page 25). This recipe was created to help add necessary, delicious fat to many of the basic meat dishes. You can add it to the raw meat dishes or to any of the grilled meats. You will love the smooth, creamy texture and delicate flavor. For this recipe, we recommend that the eggs be as fresh as possible.

2 organic egg yolks

½ tsp fine sea salt

¼ cup (56 g) Golden Marrow Fat (see page 143), melted

In a small glass bowl, place the yolks and the salt. With an electric or manual whisk, start whisking the yolks at a low speed, then start adding the fat in a slow trickle. Keep whisking until all of the fat is incorporated, then raise the speed to medium and whisk for another 30 seconds. You should have created a smooth, golden emulsion.

Place the cream in a small sealable glass jar and refrigerate it for up to 5 days.

Nutrition Notes

Raw eggs have many benefits. They contain essential nutrients for the brain, nerves, glands and hormones, they are nutritionally balanced and we highly recommend the addition of raw eggs to your nutritional program. The sulfur amino acids help to keep you young. Raw eggs also contain an abundance of other vital substances, including protein, essential fatty acids, niacin, riboflavin, biotin, choline, vitamins A, D and E, magnesium, potassium, phosphorous, manganese, iron, iodine, copper, zinc and sulfur. Egg yolks are one of the few foods that contain vitamin D.

Berry Mousse

ANCESTRAL STYLE

Yields 4 servings
Per Serving:
Calories 460
Fat 32 g
Protein 37 g
Carbs 0 g

This berry mousse can seem like a fun way to add variety to the Ancestral Style of the Carnivore diet, but it packs a nutritional punch. For those occasions when you miss a treat, the honeyed, tangy flavor of this airy mousse will hit the spot.

3 cups (720 ml) hot water
3 tbsp (30 g) beef gelatin
2 organic egg yolks
2 cups (280 g) frozen blueberries
Honey, optional

In a blender, mix the water with the gelatin on low speed. With the blender running, add the egg yolks one at a time. Blend for 1 minute, until the mixture is smooth and frothy. With the blender running, increase the speed to medium and add the frozen berries all at once. Blend for 1 minute, until a smooth foam is created. The foam should solidify pretty much immediately.

Scoop the mousse out of the blender with a spoon and serve it in bowls with a drizzle of the honey, if using.

Nutrition Notes

The Ancestral Style of the Carnivore diet enables you to use some strategic carbohydrates for quick energy before an athletic competition or for help with carb cycling. Carb cycling can help women who are perimenopausal or missing periods, as well as athletes who want to load their muscles with glycogen.

Marrow Berry Shots

ANCESTRAL STYLE

Yields 2 servings
Per Serving:
Calories 233
Fat 13 g
Protein 17 g
Carbs 12 g

Marrow berry shots give you the nutritional benefit of bone marrow with an infusion of berries. This is the perfect drink to have on a summer day, or when you're craving something with a little sweet kick. Make sure to use in-season, organic berries that have a low glycemic index. For this recipe, feel free to use chicken, beef or big game marrow bones. We have called for beef marrow bones because they are easy to find at most grocery stores. If you are having trouble finding marrow bones, ask your butcher to set some aside for you.

3 lb (1.4 kg) grass-fed beef or bison marrow bones

6 cups (1.4 L) filtered water

½ tsp fine sea salt

½ cup (60 g) raspberries

½ cup (60 g) blackberries

1 tbsp (15 ml) honey, optional

8–10 ice cubes

In a medium soup pot over medium-high heat, bring the bones, water and salt to a boil. Reduce the heat, and simmer the mixture for 35 minutes, until the bones are fully cooked and the marrow easily falls out of the bone.

Take the broth off the heat, let it cool for 20 minutes, then refrigerate it for 1 hour to cool.

Pull the bones out of the liquid and remove and reserve the excess fat and marrow from the bones; discard the bones. Using the excess fat and marrow ensures your berry shots will be as nutritionally dense as possible. Put the marrow broth, marrow and fat into a blender with the raspberries, blackberries, honey, if using, and ice. Blend for 1 minute, until all of the ingredients are blended together.

Serve in a glass. Leftovers can be stored in the refrigerator for 2 to 3 days; just make sure to shake or blend the mixture before drinking it, as the berries and fat may separate.

Nutrition Notes

This is a great treat for recovery after a workout, hard physical effort or hike or if you just feel like you need a pick-me-up. The berries provide a significant amount of antioxidants, as well as a small number of carbohydrates to give you extra energy. The bone marrow included in this recipe provides calcium, which is excellent for supporting strong bones and preventing arthritis.

Yields 2 servings
Per Serving:
Calories 192
Fat 12 g
Protein 12 g
Carbs 9 g

Collagen-Infused Immune Smoothie

ANCESTRAL STYLE

This is a high collagen content blend that will provide you with not only what will taste like a treat, but also a variety of nutrients. When shopping for marrow bones, try to source them from the highest-quality grass-fed animal you can find, as they will have the most nutrition. We have also added raspberries and orange to our immune smoothie, which contains vitamins, antioxidants and a small amount of carbohydrates.

3 lb (1.4 kg) grass-fed beef or bison marrow bones

6 cups (1.4 L) filtered water

½ tsp fine sea salt

½ cup (60 g) raspberries

½ orange, peeled

8–10 ice cubes

In a medium soup pot over medium-high heat, bring the bones, water and salt to a boil. Reduce the heat and simmer the mixture for 35 minutes, until the marrow bones are fully cooked and the marrow easily falls out of the bones.

Pull the bones out of the liquid, and remove and reserve the excess fat and marrow from the bones; discard the bones. Take the broth off the heat for 20 minutes, then refrigerate it for 1 hour to cool it.

In a blender, blend the broth, fat, marrow, raspberries, orange and ice for 40 seconds, until the ingredients are smooth and blended together. If your blender won't accommodate the amount of broth, blend half of the broth, berries and orange at a time. You can also save the other half of the broth to make a smoothie later. Marrow broth will keep in your refrigerator for up to 10 days.

Nutrition Notes

This recipe contains protein, carbohydrates and a small amount of fat, which ends up being a great macro profile for pre- and post-physical activity. The carbohydrates provided are great for getting through a workout or long day, and the protein and fat will keep you satiated. This recipe provides a significant amount of vitamin C from the berries and orange. Vitamin C helps reduce the uric acid levels in the blood and may help prevent chronic disease.

Trail Mix with Dried Steak, Coffee and Dried Fruit

ANCESTRAL STYLE

Yields 4 servings
Per Serving:
Calories 613
Fat 29 g
Protein 61 g
Carbs 27 g

Jerky is a great way to add a snack into your busy day or pack for a hike or bike ride. Since jerky is dehydrated, it can safely stay out of the refrigerator during the day. We recommend using a leaner cut of beef, such as flank steak, London Broil or New York strip.

2 lb (910 g) flank steak, cut into ½-inch (12-mm) strips

Juice of 1 orange

2 tbsp (30 ml) honey

2 tbsp (30 g) fine sea salt

¼ cup (21 g) premium coffee grounds

¼ cup (35 g) unsweetened dried cherries

¼ cup (45 g) whole dried apricots

Preheat the oven to 225°F (107°C).

In a large bowl combine the steak, orange juice, honey, salt and coffee. Place a wire drying rack on top of a baking sheet and place the steak strips on top of the rack 1 inch (2.5 cm) apart.

Bake the jerky for 3 hours, until it is dry and pulls apart easily. Turn the jerky over 90 minutes into the baking time.

Cool the jerky completely, then chop it into 1-inch (2.5-cm) pieces. In a large bowl, combine the jerky, cherries and apricots. Store the jerky in an airtight glass container.

Nutrition Notes

Homemade jerky made from grass-fed beef is packed with protein and high in omega-3 fatty acids. Dried fruit is high in fiber and provides an adequate amount of carbohydrates; when combined with coffee, this becomes a great energy source to get you through your busy day. Carbohydrates can be beneficial when used with proper food timing and, prior to training, will give you the energy that may be required to sustain a physical effort, while carbohydrates post training can aid in recovery. This is the perfect snack for hiking or backpacking, recovering from workouts or to pack in your gym bag.

Flan with Honey

ANCESTRAL STYLE

Yields 2 servings

Per Serving:
Calories 376
Fat 20 g
Protein 25 g
Carbs 24 g

Flan with honey will taste like a delicious treat compared to the savory foods you are enjoying while following this diet. This recipe is made with high-quality ingredients that will keep you on track longer if you are craving something sweet. Flan is a decadent dessert traditionally served in Spain, France, Rome and Germany. The original dish was very simple: baked eggs and milk, sometimes topped with honey. As the dish spread across Europe, different cultures adopted their own renditions. Flan tastes similar to a custard, but when it is baked it becomes firmer. Because flan is very high in protein and low in sugar, it is a great dish to have more regularly than other desserts. We recommend using high-quality honey and organic, omega-3 eggs.

12 egg whites, at room temperature

6 egg yolks, at room temperature

2 tbsp (30 ml) honey, divided

Grated zest of 1 orange

1½ tsp (9 g) coarse sea salt or kosher salt

Orange slices, for garnish

Preheat the oven to 350°F (177°C).

In a large bowl, beat the egg whites for 3 minutes, until they start to stiffen. Then fold in the yolks, 1 tablespoon (15 ml) of the honey, the orange zest and the salt. Beat the mixture on low, or slowly with a whisk, for 20 seconds, until all of the ingredients are blended together and the mixture looks like foam. Pour the mixture into a 6- to 8-inch (15- to 20-cm) glass baking dish.

Bake the flan for 50 minutes, until the sides are set but the middle is jiggly. Do not overcook; it's better to undercook than overcook. The flan will continue to cook once you remove it from the oven.

Top the flan with the remaining tablespoon (15 ml) of honey and the orange slices. The flan will stay fresh, covered in the fridge, for 2 to 3 days.

Nutrition Notes

The small amount of carbohydrates in this recipe is a great refuel for a long hike or day of exercise. While the recipe does include carbohydrates, the protein and fat are high quality and rich in omega-3. Flan is easy to digest and mellow on the gut. Omega-3 fatty acid is helpful for eye health and brain function.

Acknowledgments

Vivica

I am absolutely delighted for having had another opportunity to create with my favorite medium: food! I deeply love food, and, as a good Italian, I love feeding people. What makes me happiest is when I get to combine this creativity with a strong message of healing.

Thank you for all the trailblazers in the Carnivore community who inspired me and taught me so much: Dr. Shawn Baker, Natalie Daniels, once my client and now an esteemed colleague, Dr. Zsofia Clemens, Vanessa Spina, Caitlin Weeks and many more.

I would like to thank all the editors at Page Street Publishing for their patience and support in making this project be the best it could be!

I am grateful for my boyfriend, Benjamin, for being the best recipe tester and for providing a great kitchen to work in; thank you for all the support.

Thank you, Erin, my co-author, for being the kind, smart, talented, incredible superwoman you are. I am so happy to have created this book with you!

And, lastly, thank you to my patients, who are always my biggest teachers. I am honored to share your health journey, and I care about you!

Erin

I am extremely excited for the opportunity to co-write alongside Vivica Menegaz and Page Street Publishing on this project.

The editors at Page Street have been an awesome support in helping us use our creativity to shine new light on a very old way of eating.

Food has been my passion for as long as I can remember. My career path has grown from simply making amazing food to share with others to helping people with their health and wellness goals; it is through the stomach that we feed our soul.

I am proud to present this book, our recipes and shared knowledge, as not just a cookbook but a way-of-life book. As a former vegan athlete for over a decade, this book represents my personal growth and my long search for health and well-being. I'm very passionate about eating healthy, naturally raised, sustainable meat, and I've seen the benefits firsthand in my body's ability to heal with the Carnivore diet.

I'd like to thank Shawn Baker, Paul Saladino, Joe Rogan, Robb Wolf and the many other nutrition experts who have broadened my thinking and nutrition practice. Thank you for your influence and continued research into finding ways to improve human health.

I am extremely thankful for my husband, Michael Blevins, who has not only inspired and supported me in every aspect of my life but also pushed me to expand and grow my knowledge of nutrition and sports performance. I would also like to thank Mark Twight for showing me that effort makes all things possible; your writing moves mountains, and I respect the places you have been in your life and the lessons you've brought back to share. I'm grateful for Kegan Dillon and Josh Goldstein for sharing their personal adjustments of the Carnivore diet. I would like to thank Mike Thurk for his amazing photography and Black Rifle Coffee, Traeger Grills, Honey Beard Protein and Ancestral Supplements for the products I use daily. I really appreciate the ongoing support.

A special thank-you to my beautiful daughter, London, who has proven to be the best assistant and sous chef I've ever had. And thank you to everyone at The Non Prophet project for your constant support, critical feedback and great minds. A huge thank-you to my clients, athletes, project managers and production teams that I've worked with for trusting in me and working as hard as you do to improve yourselves. Last, I want to thank my beautiful mom, who passed away during the process of writing this book. Thank you for your encouragement.

I couldn't have done it without any of you.

About the Authors

Vivica Menegaz is the author of four published cookbooks, including *The Keto Paleo Kitchen* and *The Ultimate Paleo Cookbook*. She is a holistic practitioner who specializes in helping women heal their hormones and lose weight through the use of a therapeutic diet, combining lifestyle and mindset. Originally from Italy, Vivica has always been around food, both through her family of restaurateurs and in her early career as a food photographer. In her late thirties, she finally discovered nutrition: her true vocation. After working for five years for a chiropractic office, Vivica opened her own web-based practice, specializing in Therapeutic Ketogenic and Carnivore Diets. Vivica is the creator of The Healing Foods Method, a four-month, one-on-one course to transform health and lifestyle, with a focus on metabolism and endocrine rebalancing. The program has been extremely successful, helping hundreds of people to transform their lives and health.

Erin Blevins is the founder of shutupEAT and shutupWORK. She is a celebrity and special project private chef, a nutrition coach, a gym owner and a competitive athlete. Her work can be seen in blockbuster movies like Warner Brothers's *Justice League*, for which her nutrition and cooking helped transform actor Henry Cavill into Superman. Her work has helped in the team development for The Atlanta Braves and also on some of the steepest hills of Red Bull Rampage, with some of the world's best female downhill racers. She has helped thousands of private clients, including celebrities, professional fighters, elite ultra-marathoners, professional downhill skiers, CrossFit athletes and national record-holding weight lifters, as well as Navy SEALs and other US Special Operations Forces, take control of their diet and nutrition in order to perform, recover and live better. Her goal is to share her love of food, fitness and adventure as a tool to improve your life.

Index

F

fasting, 17, 20–21

fats, 15, 16, 25

fat-shaming, 14

fat storage, 14, 15

female hormones, 15, 18, 29

fiber, 27

fish

    Baked Rainbow Trout with Orange and Thyme, 100

    Branzino al Sale: Salt-Crusted Sea Bass, 115

    Honey-Citrus Baked Salmon, 116

    Lime Ceviche with Mango, 112

Flan with Honey, 155

G

gelatin, 18, 132

    Berry Mousse, 147

    Tongue and Marrow Broth Aspic, 44

ghee, 19, 24

ghrelin, 14

gluconeogenesis, 25

glucosamine, 143

glucose, 14, 15, 25

glycine, 143

glycogen, 14, 17, 147

gut-healing, 16, 18, 27, 28

H

histamines, 140

honey

    Flan with Honey, 155

    Honey-Citrus Baked Salmon, 116

    Honey-Glazed Beef Spareribs, 79

    Honey-Orange Pulled Wild Boar, 84

    Trail Mix with Dried Steak, Coffee and Dried Fruit, 152

hormones, 14–15, 18, 28, 29

hot flashes, 28

hypothalamus, 28

hypothyroidism, 19

I

inflammation, 24, 143

insulin, 14, 15, 18

insulin resistance, 14–15

intermittent fasting, 17, 20–21

iodine, 19

iron, 18, 47, 55, 72